AESCHYLUS EURIPIDES SOPHOCLES

The Electra Plays

Translated with Notes by Peter Meineck,

Cecelia Eaton Luschnig, and Paul Woodruff

Introduction by

Justina Gregory

Hackett Publishing Company, Inc.
Indianapolis/Cambridge

Printed in the United States of America

14 13 12 11 10 09 1 2 3 4 5 6 7

For further information, please address:

Hackett Publishing Company, Inc.
P.O. Box 44937
Indianapolis, IN 46244-0937

www.hackettpublishing.com

Cover design by Brian Rak and Abigail Coyle
Text design by Meera Dash
Composition by William Hartman
Map by William Nelson
Printed at Edwards Brothers, Inc.

Library of Congress Cataloging-in-Publication Data

Aeschylus.
[Choephori. English]
The Electra plays / Aeschylus, Euripides, Sophocles ; translated with notes by Peter Meineck, Cecelia Eaton Luschnig, and Paul Woodruff ; introduction by Justina Gregory.
p. cm.
Includes bibliographical references and index.
ISBN 978-0-87220-964-0 (pbk.) —
ISBN 978-0-87220-965-7 (cloth)
1. Electra (Greek mythology) —Drama. 2. Orestes (Greek mythology) —Drama. I. Meineck, Peter, 1967– II. Luschnig, C. A. E. III. Woodruff, Paul, 1943– IV. Euripides. Electra English. V. Sophocles. Electra English. VI. Title.

PA3643.A2E44 2009
882'.01—dc22

2008048132

The paper used in this publication meets the minimum requirements of American National Standard for Information Sciences—Permanence of Paper for Printed Library Materials, ANSI Z39.48–1984.

∞

The Electra Plays

Contents

Introduction

Dio Chrysostom, a Greek philosopher of the second century C.E., sat down after breakfast one morning to read the *Philoctetes* tragedies of Aeschylus, Sophocles, and Euripides one after the other (*Discourse* 52, trans. D. A. Russell):

> I produced the plays for myself (in my mind's eye) very splendidly, and tried to give them my full attention, like a judge of the first tragic choruses. But had I been on oath, I could never have come to a decision. So far as I was concerned, none of them could have been beaten.

It is impossible to recreate Dio Chrysostom's experience, for of the three *Philoctetes* plays only Sophocles' survives. Nor is it possible to compare the lost *Oedipus* plays of Aeschylus and Euripides to Sophocles' version, or juxtapose Aeschylus' lost *Pentheus* with Euripides' *Bacchae.* By great good fortune, however, we possess one tragedy of each poet recounting Orestes and Electra's revenge on the murderers of their father Agamemnon. The plays in question—Aeschylus' *Libation Bearers* and the *Electra* of Euripides and Sophocles, respectively—are brought together in this volume.

Each of these tragedies could profitably be read in conjunction with others by the same author: *The Libation Bearers* with Aeschylus' *Agamemnon* and *Furies,* the plays that preceded and followed it in its original production; Sophocles' *Electra* with *Antigone,* another tragedy featuring a strong, passionate female protagonist who is paired with a cautious, conformist sister; Euripides' *Electra* with *Orestes* and *Iphigenia among the Taurians,* plays which carry further the troubled history of the Atreids (that is, the descendants of Atreus). Placing *The Libation Bearers* and the two *Electras* side by side, however, yields unique benefits. There can be no question of ranking the three, for each dramatist, as Dio Chrysostom understood, has his distinct sensibility. A comparison of the three plays sets that sensibility in relief and sheds light, as well, on the dramatists' complex relationship with the literary tradition and with one another. Moreover, a comparison of the three plays demonstrates the astonishing flexibility of Greek myth. Not only can the same set of mythical events be construed as a beginning (by Euripides), a middle (by Aeschylus), and an end (by Sophocles), it can also be used to explore topics as disparate as the nature of justice (Aeschylus), divine responsibility for human misery (Euripides), and the relationship between words and deeds (Sophocles).

Historical Background

Greek tragedy is indelibly associated with a particular place, occasion, and historical moment. Although revivals of tragedy would eventually be staged all over the Greek-speaking world, most plays had their initial production in Athens at the dramatic competition of the City Dionysia, a spring festival honoring the god Dionysus with sacrifices, processions, and performances. And although tragedies would continue to be composed in the fourth century B.C.E., thirty-one of the thirty-two plays that have survived are from the fifth century. The extraordinary flowering of tragic drama that is associated with the names of Aeschylus (c. 525–456 B.C.E.), Sophocles (c. 496–405 B.C.E.), and Euripides (c. 484–406 B.C.E.) is bracketed by the Persian Wars between Greece and Persia on one side and the Peloponnesian War between Athens and Sparta on the other. Tragedy is not an overtly political genre, and only rarely do the dramatists allude to major historical developments of this period, such as the evolution of Athenian democracy and the expansion of Athens' empire. The sociopolitical issues associated with these developments, however—for example, the role of the state in administering justice, or the relationship between individual and community—are omnipresent in Greek tragedy. Athenian democracy required the participation of the entire male citizenry, and tragedy, it would appear, was regarded as an ideal vehicle for exposing the Athenians to moral and ethical complexities they would necessarily confront in the discharge of their democratic responsibilities.

How and why did tragedy come to fill this role? For the Athenians tragedy was mass entertainment; everyone could enjoy its exciting plots (featuring themes like adultery, betrayal, murder, deception, revenge); its expressive masks and elaborate costumes; its lavish use of music, song, and dance. Tragedy exerted its influence by emotional, visual, and auditory, as well as intellectual, means. The ambience was decidedly popular: ancient audiences viewed the plays in an open-air theater designed to accommodate at least fifteen thousand spectators and situated in the heart of civic and religious Athens. (Early performances took place in the marketplace. Later a theater was built into the southern slope of the Acropolis—the same site that a later theater still occupies today.)

The Context of Production

The City Dionysia combined religious celebration with civic oversight. The plays were presented under the auspices of the god Dionysus, but it was a polis official, the eponymous archon, who drew up the program six months in advance, choosing three dramatists who would compete for first, second, or third prize as determined by a panel of citizen judges. Each drama was presented at the Dionysia once only, although repeat performances may subsequently have taken place in the rural communities surrounding Athens. The tragedies of Aeschylus, exceptionally, became something of a dramatic staple: after his death the Athenians passed a decree authorizing revivals of his plays.

Each dramatist presented not a single play but a tetralogy, a program of three tragedies followed by a satyr-play. Satyr-plays, named after the half-human, half-bestial followers of Dionysus who comprised the chorus, offered what we would call "comic relief" after the serious matter of the tragedies. Satyr-plays were generically and tonally distinct, however, from comedies (which were also presented at the City Dionysia, although they were more closely associated with a winter festival, the Lenaea). Tragedians (for example, Aeschylus, Sophocles, and Euripides) were expected to compose both tragedies and satyr-plays, but comedy was the purview of other dramatists (for example, Aristophanes, Eupolis, and Cratinus). Both tragedies and satyr-plays derived their subject matter largely from myth, but tragedy treated the mythical material seriously while satyr-play gave it a burlesque and ribald spin. The plots of comedy, in contrast, featured invented characters and situations that combined high fantasy with transparent references to contemporary Athens. Satyr-plays honored the festival setting by bringing Dionysiac elements to the fore; they also served as a counterpoint to the tragedies that preceded them, providing "liberation and emotional relaxation" (Seidensticker 2005, p. 48) and allowing the spectators to leave the theater in high spirits even as they continued to ponder the implications of the tragedies they had seen earlier in the day.

The system of financing for the plays confirms their tangible value to the polis. Tragedies were expensive to produce. To be sure, they did not require elaborate sets: a simple wooden building, the *skēnē,* could stand for tomb, palace, hut, or any other structure required by the action, and much was left to verbal description and to the spectators' imagination. There were, however, considerable expenses associated with the cast. Two or three professional male actors, trained to play multiple characters and to assume both male and female roles, were required for each tragedy; the polis met the costs of their salary. But each play also demanded, at a minimum, a chorus of nonprofessional singers and dancers (twelve in number until Sophocles raised it to fifteen) and a musician who accompanied the lyric passages on the double pipe. Additionally, a tragedy might call for extras who did not have speaking parts but who still needed to be rehearsed and provided with masks and costumes. The same archon who selected the festival program designated a *chorēgos* for each tetralogy, a wealthy private citizen who was charged with assembling a chorus for each play and paying its expenses. The *chorēgos* undertook this organizational and financial responsibility as a public service; subsidizing a tetralogy counted as a contribution of the same order as other polis expenses financed by donation, such as outfitting a warship or maintaining the athletes who were training for the Panhellenic games. In recognition of his sponsorship, the *chorēgos* shared in the honor if his playwright was awarded first prize.

The City Dionysia was the most inclusive event of the Athenian year. Most Athenian institutions, whether civic or religious, were segregated: the political assembly, for example, was open only to male Athenian citizens, while certain religious festivals were reserved for women. The dramatic performances were exceptional: while the male citizenry undoubtedly constituted the target audience, other groups were not excluded. (Some scholars maintain that the dramatic performances were not open to women, but there is no ancient statement to that effect and considerable evidence pointing in the opposite direction; see Csapo and Slater 1995, pp. 286–92.) It appears that the theater was at least theoretically open to all: men, women, and children; aristocrats, commoners, and slaves; poor and wealthy; city-dwellers and farmers; Athenians, foreigners resident in Athens, and visitors from abroad.

The polis did all it could to encourage attendance. Probably as early as the fifth century, a civic fund subsidized the cost of admission. Prisoners were released on bail for the five days of the festival; as a further inducement to attend, all city business was suspended. The Athenians regarded the offerings at the City Dionysia as a vehicle for education as well as for entertainment; as the comic poet Aristophanes observes in a rare moment of seriousness, a tragedian is to be admired for his "skillfulness and admonitions, and because [he] improve[s] / men in the cities" (Aristophanes, *Frogs* 1009–10)—improves them, that is, in the exercise of their civic capacities.

The formative role Aristophanes attributes to tragedy is consistent with Greek cultural assumptions about the function of poetry. Poetry, especially Homeric epic, was traditionally regarded as an authoritative source of cultural and ethical instruction; as Aristophanes additionally observes, "For children / it is the schoolteacher who instructs; for young men it is the poets" (Aristophanes, *Frogs* 1054–55). Tragic instruction does not, however, take the form of potted commandments or prohibitions. Instead tragedy unfolds the full complexity of a mythical event, leaving it to the individual spectators to think through the issues presented on stage and draw their own analogies between the mythical past and the fifth-century present.

The Mythical Background

There was no canonical version of any Greek myth; instead poets and visual artists produced many competing variations. A poet could not alter a myth's fundamental core, but he could depart from previous versions by making changes that cumulatively modified its tendency. A poet could sketch in an alternative backstory; transpose, downplay, or suppress certain elements; change the locale; alter, omit, or combine existing characters and even invent new ones. The following events are fundamental to the story of the house of Atreus: Agamemnon's father Atreus quarrels with his brother Thyestes and serves him his own children's flesh at a banquet; Thyestes curses his brother's line; Agamemnon assents to the sacrifice of his daughter Iphigenia so the Greek fleet can sail to Troy; Clytemnestra and her lover Aegisthus, Thyestes' only surviving son, murder Agamemnon upon his return from the Trojan War; Agamemnon's son Orestes comes back from exile to kill his father's murderers. Each of these incidents, however, can acquire a very different resonance depending on context, tone, and selection of details. For the story of Orestes, Aeschylus, Sophocles, and Euripides could draw on two divergent traditions, one commending Orestes as a glorious hero and the other emphasizing the terrible consequences of his deed.

Homer

Agamemnon's homecoming is evoked throughout Homer's *Odyssey* as "both a parallel and a contrast with [the] main theme of the return of Odysseus" (Garvie 1986, p. ix). The two heroes' wives—the adulterous Clytemnestra, the faithful Penelope—could hardly be more different. A contrasting reception awaits each hero on his return from Troy: Clytemnestra plots with Aegisthus to murder Agamemnon whereas Penelope, once convinced of her husband's identity, welcomes him with open arms. Yet each hero has a son who is duty bound to avenge his father and reclaim his own stolen patrimony. When the goddess Athena urges Odysseus' son Telemachus to think about killing his mother's suitors, she adduces Orestes as an exemplar: "Haven't you heard how Orestes won glory / throughout the world when he killed Aegisthus, / the shrewd traitor who murdered his father?" (*Odyssey* 1.298–300).

Homer must choose his details carefully to arrive at this celebratory portrayal of Orestes. To be sure, a Greek audience would have no doubt that Orestes' killing of Aegisthus was right and proper. *Dikē,* the Greek word for justice, also signifies (among a constellation of other meanings) punishment, retribution, and revenge. Justice is traditionally equated with retaliation in kind: "Help your friends, harm your enemies" is a fundamental rule of Greek ethics (see Whitlock Blundell 1989, pp. 26–31). All the same, the Homeric Orestes gets off surprisingly lightly. Murderers were generally believed to incur blood-guilt requiring ceremonial purification, but we hear nothing of lingering pollution in his case. Moreover, a second fundamental rule of Greek ethics states that one must honor the gods, strangers, and one's parents. Although Orestes killed not only Aegisthus but also his mother Clytemnestra, this fact goes unmentioned here and elsewhere in the poem. Clytemnestra's death is acknowledged at *Odyssey* 3.309–10, when Nestor mentions the funeral banquet arranged by Orestes to commemorate "his hateful mother and her craven lover," but Nestor does not say how she died. Homer's silence does not mean that he is ignorant of the tradition that Orestes murdered Clytemnestra; rather, he suppresses that element as unsuitable to his narrative purpose. Orestes as Aegisthus' rightful killer makes a glorious example for Athena to hold up to Telemachus; Orestes as matricide would confuse Telemachus and the audience alike.

Stesichorus

The death of Agamemnon was a popular topic for vase painters in the sixth and fifth centuries (see Garvie 1986, pp. xxii–xxiv); we hear also of other literary versions, now mostly lost. Only a few fragments survive of the *Oresteia* of Stesichorus, a sixth-century B.C.E. lyric poet, but they hint at a much darker interpretation than Homer's. Stesichorus' Clytemnestra was evidently more active and more brutal than the Clytemnestra of the *Odyssey*. One fragment (Fragment 219 Davies) describes her dream of a bloodied snake, which can only represent Agamemnon; if Clytemnestra is haunted by this ominous dream it must have been she, not Aegisthus as in Homer, who assumed the leading role in the murder.

Stesichorus' *Oresteia* was a poem in two books—lengthy enough to accommodate an expanded cast of characters. One of these characters was Orestes' nurse; we can surmise that (as recounted in Pindar, *Pythian* 11.17–18) she spirited the boy out of the country after Agamemnon's death to be raised by a family friend. The nurse's intervention suggests that Stesichorus' Clytemnestra not only murdered her husband but also posed a threat to her son.

Stesichorus' version also included Electra—not mentioned in Homer—as a leading character. A papyrus fragment (Fragment 217 Davies) mentions "recognition via the lock of hair" as a feature of his poem—the first appearance of the reunion of brother and sister that will become a feature of all three tragedies. Finally, Stesichorus introduced divine characters into his narrative. In

Homer's version the characters initiate action on their own without the prompting of the gods; Aegisthus, indeed, murders Agamemnon in defiance of divine warnings (see *Odyssey* 1.35–43). Stesichorus' poem, however, featured divinities who intervened both to help and to harm Orestes. Apollo extended tangible protection after the murders, offering Orestes a bow made of horn to defend himself against his mother's Furies. The Furies—chthonic avengers of wrongdoing, especially of crimes against parents—here make their first attested appearance in the myth; they both signify and respond to the horror of the matricide. Whether or not these motifs originated with Stesichorus, his poem seems to have been the conduit that transmitted them to the three dramatists.

Aeschylus

Most tragedians chose a different myth for each of the three tragedies they presented at the City Dionysia. Aeschylus, however, often preferred to present successive episodes from a single myth in "a narratively connected unit with a continuous plot" (Gantz 1980, p. 133). Even the satyr-play drew on related subject matter. In 458 B.C.E., Aeschylus presented three tragedies tracing the vicissitudes of the house of Atreus through two cycles of crime and punishment, and incorporating allusions to earlier crimes that suggest a family curse operating over generations. The satyr-play *Proteus,* now lost, staged the encounter in Egypt of Agamemnon's brother Menelaus and Proteus, the old man of the sea (for the story, see *Odyssey* 4.351–570).

The overarching theme of Aeschylus' *Oresteia* is the difficult search for *dikē*. This theme is not inevitably associated with the myth of the Atreids; for Homer, as we have noted, Orestes' deed was a source of simple glory. The multigenerational sweep of Aeschylus' trilogy, however, brings clearly into view two problems that arise when the traditional understanding of *dikē* as retaliatory justice is brought to bear on the story of the Atreids. First, each act of revenge brings another in its wake, setting up an unending cycle of suffering and retribution. Second, Apollo's command that Orestes should kill his mother collides head-on with the obligation to honor one's parents.

Agamemnon, the first play of the *Oresteia* trilogy, dramatizes Agamemnon's return from Troy and his murder by Clytemnestra, acting in consort with Aegisthus. Clytemnestra's action is overdetermined; as she herself explains, she is avenging the sacrifice of Iphigenia (*Agamemnon,* abbreviated here as *Ag.*, 1415–18, 1524–26), she is angry at Agamemnon's adultery with the Trojan priestess Cassandra (*Ag.* 1438–43; she does not mention her own adulterous relationship with Aegisthus), and she is driven by "the age-old spirit of vengeance" (*Ag.* 1499, trans. P. Meineck) that haunts the house. Aegisthus has his own separate motive: since Atreus himself is dead, he can only avenge his father Thyestes' wrongs on Atreus' son Agamemnon (*Ag.* 1580–82). Clytemnestra believes or at least hopes that Agamemnon's death will bring the family troubles to an end. In the last lines of the play she reassures Aegisthus, "You and I hold / the power of this house. We will set things right once and for / all" (*Ag.* 1670–72).

The Libation Bearers proves her wrong as it presents the reciprocal murder of Aegisthus and Clytemnestra by Orestes, acting in consort with Electra. Orestes, like his mother, explains his motives (*The Libation Bearers,* abbreviated here as *LB,* 269–304). He feels an obligation, reinforced by divine threats, to avenge his father's murder; he needs to reclaim the inheritance stolen by Clytemnestra and Aegisthus; he wants to free the people of Argos from their unlawful rulers. But even though his motives are sound, and even though Clytemnestra deserves to die for her crimes, Orestes' act awakens his mother's Furies. They duly arrive at the end of the play, driving Orestes offstage and out of Argos.

The Furies, the last play of the trilogy, recounts Orestes' flight to Athens, where he stands trial with the Furies as his accusers and Apollo as his defender in an Athenian law court established by Athena to try homicide cases in perpetuity. This judicial innovation not only results in acquittal for Orestes but also makes homicide the responsibility of the polis; no longer will the family members of a murder victim be obligated to repay blood with blood. Because *The Libation Bearers* is situated at the midpoint of the arc of events traced by the trilogy, any consideration of the play must take its central position into account.

The Libation Bearers immediately declares its connection with the preceding play. The setting is Agamemnon's tomb, where Orestes is dedicating a lock of hair to his father's ghost. Orestes' return from exile, in any case a staple of the myth, was foreshadowed at the end of *Agamemnon* when the chorus of old men of Argos prayed openly and defiantly that Orestes would come back to kill their tyrannical rulers (*Ag.* 1646–48). His presence at the tomb makes it immediately clear that Clytemnestra was indulging in wishful thinking when she reassured Aegisthus that with Agamemnon dead all would be well.

The next to arrive at Agamemnon's tomb is Electra; accompanying her is the chorus of Eastern slave women, the "libation bearers" of the play's title. Clytemnestra has entrusted the women with liquid offerings intended to placate Agamemnon's ghost, but Electra is hesitant to carry out her mother's orders. She understands that it is a travesty of piety to pour libations on behalf of the murderer at her victim's tomb, and wants to turn the offerings to her own advantage. The chorus leader helps her find the appropriate words for her prayer, but the focus of the scene then shifts as Electra notices "something new" (*LB* 166) on the tomb—Orestes' lock of hair.

At this point we can see how Aeschylus borrows motifs from Stesichorus' *Oresteia* and adapts them to his own purposes. For Stesichorus, the recognition between Orestes and Electra hinged on a lock of Orestes' hair. Aeschylus multiplies the tokens to produce a tense and psychologically rich recognition scene. Electra notices that the lock of hair is identical to her own, but assumes that Orestes has sent it rather than dedicating it in person. Next she spots two sets of footprints and realizes that one set matches her own. This sign, suggestive of her brother's actual presence, sends her into a frenzy of suspense, which Orestes cuts short by emerging from hiding and identifying himself. Electra does not immediately believe him, but Orestes produces a piece of weaving made by Electra in her childhood and retained by Orestes during his years of exile. This token clinches the recognition.

This scene will come under withering criticism from Euripides' *Electra* because of its implausibility. Euripides' *Electra* points out that men's hair has a different texture from women's, and that strangers can share the same hair color; that dry ground cannot register footprints, and that men have larger feet than women; and that clothing woven for a child would not fit an adult (Euripides' *Electra,* abbreviated here as E. *El.,* 524–44). Realism, however, is not Aeschylus' concern in this scene. Rather, Electra's instantaneous grasp of the significance of the tokens suggests an instinctive sympathy between sister and brother, a sympathy that contrasts with Clytemnestra's subsequent failure to recognize her son when he is standing right in front of her.

Recognition shades into prayer as Orestes implores Zeus to look favorably on their project and describes the appalling punishments threatened by Apollo's oracle at Delphi if he should fail to exact retribution for his father's murder: he will incur leprosy, will experience visitations of his father's Furies, and will be shunned by all (*LB* 269–96). But Orestes also has faith that "the great oracle of Apollo will never betray me" (269), a faith he reaffirms at the end of the play (*LB* 1031). In Stesichorus, Apollo's protection seems to have been limited to a single object, the bow made of horn; in Aeschylus, Apollo plays a more expansive role, both prescribing the murder beforehand and defending Orestes in the aftermath. Apollo's patronage suggests that the matricide is more than a private family matter. Indeed, according to the chorus Zeus and Destiny—not Apollo alone—authorize Clytemnestra's murder (*LB* 306–7).

In a scene I will return to, Orestes, Electra, and the chorus engage in a joint *kommos* (ritual lament) at the tomb. Orestes then hears of the terrifying dream that inspired Clytemnestra's libations: she dreamed that she gave birth to a snake and put it to her breast, where it bit her and drew blood (*LB* 527–34). Once more Aeschylus adapts a motif from Stesichorus' *Oresteia*. In that poem Clytemnestra's dream of a bloodied snake conveyed her torment over the past; this dream, in which the snake is the aggressor rather than the victim and stands for Orestes rather than Agamemnon, both attests to her fearful state of mind and functions as a symbolic precursor of the murder.

Aeschylus probably derived the character of Orestes' nurse from Stesichorus, but he amplifies her role much as he does Apollo's. In *Agamemnon,* Clytemnestra, welcoming her husband home, explained that she herself (not the nurse, as in Stesichorus' *Oresteia*) had sent Orestes out of the country from fear of political unrest (*Ag.* 876–80). This action suggests a Clytemnestra who, in contrast to Stesichorus', is capable of maternal feeling. Indeed, when Clytemnestra receives the false news of Orestes' death in *The Libation Bearers* her reaction is ambivalent (*LB* 691–99); Aeschylus leaves it open whether she is feigning grief or is genuinely shaken. Whichever the case, the nurse (who is too lowly to be assigned a proper name; "Cilissa" means simply "the woman from Cilicia") demonstrates a profound maternal bond with Orestes. She is devastated by the report of his death, and her homely, garrulous reminiscences of looking after Orestes as a baby strike a note of unmistakable sincerity. The nurse, the spectators may well conclude, is Orestes' real mother if the criteria are tendance and affection. When Clytemnestra subsequently bares her breasts to her son as she begs him to spare her life, her gesture will mean less to the spectators because of the nurse's speech.

If Aeschylus derives some of his most striking motifs from Stesichorus, he also introduces parallels and inversions that link *The Libation Bearers* to *Agamemnon*. At the opening of the play, for example, an unforeseen resemblance emerges between Orestes and Aegisthus. Aegisthus was raised in exile and returned to Argos to avenge his father Thyestes (*Ag*. 1607). Now Orestes, also reared abroad, has returned on his own mission of vengeance. This parallel suggests that the murder of Agamemnon and the proposed murder of Aegisthus and Clytemnestra are more similar than different—each retaliatory, each justified in some ways and unjustified in others, each entailing additional suffering for the royal family and people of Argos.

Ritual is central to *The Libation Bearers,* and Aeschylus exploits it to hint at disquieting similarities between past and present. His Clytemnestra characteristically misuses religious ritual and religious language. The first the audience hears of Clytemnestra in *Agamemnon* is that she has "order[ed] sacrifices throughout the city" (*Ag*. 88). Ostensibly these are thank-offerings for the capture of Troy; in actuality she is praying for the success of her murderous scheme. When Agamemnon returns, Clytemnestra offers him a lavish welcome, then snares him in a woven net as he relaxes in his bath; subsequently she kills Cassandra, the mistress he brought back from Troy. She gloatingly describes Agamemnon's end to the appalled chorus:

> This was my work, I do not deny it,
> he could not have escaped his destiny.
> I cast my vast net, tangling around him,
> wrapping him in a robe rich in evil.
> I struck him twice and he screamed twice,
> his limbs buckled and his body came crashing down,
> and as he lay there, I struck him again, a third blow
> for Underworld Zeus, the savior of the dead.
> (*Ag*. 1380–87)

Clytemnestra's words are overtly sacrilegious. "Agamemnon's blood is a libation, and with the three strokes she gave him, each one drenching her in blood, she makes precise allusion to the customary rite of pouring three libations after the feast" (Zeitlin 1965, p. 473). But in *The Libation Bearers* Orestes echoes her language; he describes Aegisthus' death, following the butchering of Thyestes' children and the murder of Agamemnon, as a third libation: "The Fury, with its unquenchable thirst for death, / will drain a third cup of thick, pure blood" (*LB* 577–78). Upon hearing this language the spectators may reflect that Orestes has more in common with his mother than he knows.

Symmetries of staging reinforce the similarity between the two acts of vengeance. In both plays the *skēnē* represents Agamemnon's palace. Its central door is a focal point of the first play, above all when Clytemnestra entices Agamemnon inside to his death. The first half of *The Libation Bearers* takes place at Agamemnon's tomb, probably represented by an altar in the middle of the *orchēstra* (dancing area); but from the moment Orestes knocks at the palace doors (*LB* 651), the spectators' attention is again focused on the *skēnē*. At the end of *Agamemnon* Clytemnestra appeared on the *ekkyklēma* (a movable platform that could be wheeled out the door of the *skēnē*) standing above the bodies of Agamemnon and Cassandra. At the end of *The Libation Bearers* Orestes appears on the *ekkyklēma* standing above the bodies of Clytemnestra and Aegisthus. As a further visual reminder of the terrible past, he displays the net in which his mother entrapped Agamemnon.

The imagery of *The Libation Bearers* reinforces the links between past and present. Of the many images and metaphors that weave an intricate pattern through the trilogy (see Fowler 1967, Lebeck 1971), I have space to mention only one. Clytemnestra was described in *Agamemnon* as a "snake with venom at both ends" (*Ag.* 1233). Electra and Orestes echo the characterization when they imagine themselves as "the brood bereft of their eagle sire, / who died entwined in the coils of a vicious viper" (*LB* 247–48). After the murder Orestes describes his mother as "a deadly serpent, a venomous viper" (*LB* 994) and the women of the chorus appropriate the image, referring to Clytemnestra and Aegisthus as "two snakes" (*LB* 1047). The snake imagery is not limited to the usurpers, however. After hearing the description of Clytemnestra's nightmare Orestes confidently explicates its meaning: "As she has raised this gruesome omen, / so she must die. I am the snake, / I will be the one to kill her and fulfill this dream" (*LB* 548–50; compare *LB* 928). While Orestes' interpretation emphasizes his resolve, it also draws attention to the resemblance between son and mother.

The Libation Bearers also anticipates *The Furies*. As Electra struggles to articulate an appropriate prayer at her father's tomb, the chorus leader tells her to "pray that some spirit or a man may one day come," and Electra asks, "Do you mean to judge or to exact justice?" (*LB* 119–20)—a hint that the resolution to the family troubles will substitute civic process for private revenge. The very bleakness of the second play lays the groundwork for the third. In the last lines of *The Libation Bearers* Orestes has been driven from Argos as a polluted fugitive, and the women of the chorus express their despair: "When will it end? When will it be calm? / When will it sleep, this fury, this Ruin?" The end they long for will arrive in *The Furies*, as punishment for homicide becomes the responsibility of the polis. This outcome is not reached simply or easily, and spectators will have lingering doubts about the fairness of Orestes' trial, but what matters is that a solution *is* found, the impasse of *The Libation Bearers* resolved.

It would be a misconception to regard *The Libation Bearers* as merely the hinge of the *Oresteia* trilogy, for the play offers its own amendments to the theology of *Agamemnon* and introduces its own memorable effects of stagecraft. In the first play of the trilogy retaliatory justice seemed a straightforward matter: "Revenge will come and you will pay, blow for blow" (*Ag.* 1430). *The Libation Bearers* echoes this formulation: "Justice screams / and demands her price. / Bloody blow pays bloody / blow. 'The doer suffers,' / sounds the saying, three times old" (*LB* 309–12). In the course of *The Libation Bearers,* however, the characters register increasing insight into the complexities of retaliatory justice (Dodds 1960, p. 30). Orestes understands that vengeance will compound rather than correct the prior wrong: he tells his mother, "You should not have killed, now suffer what you should not" (*LB* 930). Whereas Clytemnestra in *Agamemnon* exulted in her crime and imagined that henceforth all would be well, Orestes realizes that he has "won a tainted victory" (*LB* 1017) and confesses, "I do not know how it will end" (*LB* 1021). The spectators have the opportunity to refine their own understanding along with the characters' until they too recognize that retaliatory justice is no solution.

Aeschylus directed and acted in his own plays, and he is a master at creating meaning through spectacle and stage action. *The Libation Bearers* includes four suspenseful scenic moments. The first is the three-way *kommos* at Agamemnon's tomb. The ritual lament is necessary because the murdered Agamemnon was "denied his wake" (*LB* 432), but in addition to making amends the mourners hope to raise Agamemnon's ghost. Ghostly visitations were not unknown on the Greek stage: in Aeschylus' earlier tragedy *The Persians,* for example, the ghost of King Darius rose from his tomb when summoned by the chorus. Throughout the lament, therefore, the spectators will be in suspense: will Agamemnon's ghost appear or won't he? In the end he does not, but the *kommos* is no less powerful for that. Orestes acknowledges his wretched situation ("helpless, homeless, and shamed," *LB* 408) and affirms his intention to kill his mother: "I will do away with her, then I can die" (*LB* 438). Brother, sister, and chorus end the lament in solidarity, prepared to put the murder plot into action.

Orestes' plan is simple, as he says (*LB* 554); indeed, it is too simple, for at two critical junctures an outsider must intervene to ensure its success. Although it is unusual for the choruses of Greek tragedy to take action on their own, the chorus leader asks the nurse to make sure that Aegisthus arrives without his bodyguard (*LB* 770–73). Orestes and Pylades are thus able to dispatch him without interference, but the shouts of Aegisthus' servant bring Clytemnestra to the scene. Clytemnestra first calls for an axe and then attempts persuasion, baring her breasts to her son as a reminder that she gave him life and nurture. This powerful visual appeal makes Orestes hesitate: "Pylades, what should I do? How can I kill my own mother?" (*LB* 899).

These questions cannot but take the spectators by surprise because to this point Pylades has not spoken a word. To an audience of experienced theatergoers his silence would suggest that he was a mute extra and that *The Libation Bearers* was a traditional tragedy involving two speaking actors on stage at one time—not one of the three-actor plays pioneered by Sophocles, Aeschylus' younger rival. But after Aegisthus' murder there is a change in the pattern of speakers. First the servant—a third speaking actor—rushes out of the *skēnē* to announce Aegisthus' death; then Pylades finds his voice and in the play's second powerful intervention reminds Orestes that Apollo, speaking through his oracle at Delphi, authorized and indeed demanded the murder. Whichever way this scene was originally staged—whether the slave rushed back inside and made a lightning change of mask and costume to emerge as Pylades, or whether Pylades was played by a fourth actor (see Taplin 1977, pp. 353–54)—this is an extraordinary moment theatrically and psychologically: "We see [Pylades] no longer as Orestes' inseparable companion, but as the spokesman of Apollo. It is as if the god himself had suddenly appeared" (Garvie 1986, p. l). Indeed, Pylades' timely reminder is all Orestes requires to carry through the matricide.

The fourth scenic effect involves Clytemnestra's Furies. Like Agamemnon's ghost, they make their mark by *not* appearing; or rather, they are visible to Orestes alone. When Orestes cries, "You can't see them, but I can, they force me away! / I must go now! Now!" (*LB* 1061–62), there is no suggestion that the Furies are a delusion of Orestes' deranged mind. After all, the Furies will constitute the chorus in the next play; it would be perverse for Aeschylus to suggest that they are imaginary in one play and assign them major roles in the next. Rather, they are visible only to Orestes because their business is only with him. Their presence conveys both his isolation and the insoluble dilemma he has faced from the outset: he will be persecuted by Agamemnon's Furies if he does not avenge his father, and persecuted by Clytemnestra's Furies if he does. Whichever course Orestes chooses is simultaneously right and wrong, justified and unjustifiable—a tension that persists throughout the play. Resolution will arrive in *The Furies* with Orestes' acquittal, but it is a resolution that will raise as many questions for the spectators as it answers.

Euripides

We do not have any external testimony to the date of Euripides' *Electra*. Scholars have been able to establish a chronology for the extant plays of Euripides, however, by statistical analysis of metrical patterns; this analysis yields approximate years of production for the undated plays relative to those that are securely dated. By metrical criteria *Electra* falls "between 422 and 417, with 420/19 the most likely [date]" (Cropp 1988, p. li). In terms of style, too, *Electra* is a good fit with other Euripidean tragedies belonging to this period.

What we would really like to know is whether the play preceded or followed Sophocles' *Electra*. That play is also undated, but it has structural and stylistic elements in common with other tragedies produced in the years preceding Sophocles' death in 405 (Finglass 2007, p. 1). The chronological relationship of the two *Electra*s is one of the great puzzles of classical scholarship. No consensus has emerged or is likely to, for there are plausible arguments to be made on both sides. I believe that Euripides' *Electra* came first not only on metrical and stylistic grounds, but also because the play engages so closely with Aeschylus' *Oresteia*. This assumption will guide my discussion of the two tragedies.

Euripides could have become familiar with *The Libation Bearers* in three ways. He probably attended the original performance of the *Oresteia* in 458. Play scripts were in circulation during the fifth century. And, as noted earlier, after Aeschylus' death the Athenians passed a decree authorizing revivals of his works. If (as some Aristophanic references suggest) the *Oresteia* was revived at some point in the 420s, Euripides would have had a second opportunity to watch the play; more importantly, he would have been able to count on at least some of the spectators having seen it as well, and thus appreciating his own play's dialogue with *The Libation Bearers*.

The Euripidean Electra's criticism of the Aeschylean tokens has been condemned as irrelevant, spurious—or both—by scholars (for example, Bain 1977) who do not realize that it alerts the spectators to the play's pointed critique—occasionally sly and humorous, more often passionate and intense—of Aeschylus. Euripides is not the only playwright who engages in intertextual dialogue with his fellow dramatists. We have seen Aeschylus' pointed experiment in *The Libation Bearers* with the three-actor scene introduced by Sophocles. At the opening of Sophocles' *Electra* Orestes is tempted to eavesdrop on Electra's laments, but the Tutor rejects the proposal as ill-timed (Sophocles' *Electra,* abbreviated here as S. *El.,* 80–85). The Tutor appears to be finding fault less with Orestes than with Aeschylus and Euripides, who incorporate eavesdropping scenes into *The Libation Bearers* and *Electra* respectively (Davies 1998, p. 398). All three tragedians are able to introduce an occasional in-joke without compromising the dramatic illusion or interrupting the dramatic flow.

Lacking a date of production, we also lack the titles of the other tragedies presented along with *Electra.* We can be certain, however, that the play was not part of a connected trilogy in the manner of Aeschylus. Faced with the necessity of supplying extensive background information and laying out his characters' futures within the space of a single play, Euripides has recourse to a prologue at the opening and a deus ex machina (god from the machine) at the close.

Euripides characteristically opens his tragedies with a speech by a character either directly or tangentially involved in the action who speaks to the audience with no pretense of verisimilitude, setting out essential background information and sometimes affording a glimpse of developments to follow. The prologue of *Electra* essentially summarizes Aeschylus' *Agamemnon,* adding the innovative detail that Electra has been married off to the speaker, a poor but honest farmer so awed by his wife's superior status that he has refrained from consummating the marriage. At the close of the play, as is also characteristic of Euripides, a deus ex machina provides the resolution. A crane lifts a divinity (in *Electra,* twin divinities) to the roof of the *skēnē,* from which exalted position the divinity ties up the loose ends of the plot and predicts the future. In *Electra,* Castor's prophecy encapsulates the material covered in the last play of Aeschylus' trilogy while additionally predicting that Electra will marry Pylades and that the Farmer will emigrate to Phocis and receive monetary compensation for his ordeal.

In between the prologue and the deus ex machina, *Electra* covers the same ground as Aeschylus' *Libation Bearers;* but, as will be immediately apparent to the spectators, the material has been transposed into a different key. Critics (for example, Goff 1999–2000) often emphasize the domestic and realistic atmosphere of Euripides' tragedy as compared to Aeschylus', but that is hardly a crucial difference. After all, *The Libation Bearers* includes the nurse's reminiscences of tending the infant Orestes, which take domestic detail further than any other scene in Greek tragedy. Other contrasts run deeper. Whereas Aeschylus uses parallels and inversions to place Orestes and Electra on a par with Aegisthus and Clytemnestra, Euripides emphasizes the fragility of the younger pair; they are the vulnerable offspring of the heroic generation that went off to war. Whereas Aeschylus links the family's troubles to an inherited curse, Euripides provides no such unifying explanation. Whereas Aeschylus portrays Apollo's involvement as validating the matricide, Euripides portrays it as casting doubt on the god's judgment.

For spectators with the Aeschylean version in mind, the title already bespeaks a shift: Euripides has promoted Electra to a major character (although Sophocles will give her an even more dominant role), and diminished the role of the chorus—a diminution characteristic, in fact, of later tragedy in general. The prologue makes it clear that the setting too has undergone a change: the *skēnē* now represents not the palace of Agamemnon but the country cottage where Electra, married off to a poor farmer to prevent her from bearing noble heirs, lives with her husband. This displacement is in part a literary allusion to Homer's *Odyssey,* "the prototype of all Greek stories involving return, recognition and revenge" (Davidson 1988, p. 52). In that poem, Odysseus' plot to kill the suitors is launched from his faithful swineherd's rustic hut, and at the end of the poem Odysseus is reunited with his aged father, who is leading a reduced life deep in the country. In the Odyssean tradition evoked by Euripides, a rustic setting connotes less idyllic simplicity than loss of wealth, status, and community—all associations relevant to Euripides' Electra.

The change of setting involves additional displacements. First, it entails adjustments to the murder plot, which is considerably more complex than in *The Libation Bearers.* Since Orestes cannot enter the well-guarded city (E. *El.* 615–17), the conspirators need to lure the victims outside the walls. As luck would have it, Aegisthus journeys into the countryside of his own accord, but Clytemnestra must be enticed to Electra's cottage by an elaborate deception. That she comes with kindly intent and out of pity for her daughter does not make the matricide easier for the spectators.

Another consequence of the changed setting is that the murders are no longer visually linked to the spot where Agamemnon fell. When the tableau made memorable by *The Libation Bearers* and *Agamemnon* is evoked at the end of Euripides' *Electra,* and Orestes and Electra appear on the *ekkyklēma* standing over the bodies of their mother and her lover, the visual reminiscence suggests not symmetry but a lack of correspondence between this murder and the earlier one, and makes the matricide appear more arbitrary and less justified.

The minor characters of *Electra* set in relief Euripides' modifications to the major ones. The role of the Old Man is reminiscent of the nurse in Stesichorus: he too is a devoted family retainer who spirited young Orestes out of the country at the time of Agamemnon's death. It is he who takes the lead both in identifying Orestes and in developing the murder plot; his resolve points a contrast between Euripides' hesitant Orestes and his confident counterpart in *The Libation Bearers.* As the time for the matricide approaches, Orestes berates Apollo for his "total lack of wisdom" (E. *El.* 971) and foresees that he will be polluted by the murder. The glimpse of Clytemnestra approaching at a distance causes him to doubt the legitimacy of the Delphic oracle: "Did an avenging demon speak in the guise of the god?" (E. *El.* 979). In the aftermath of the matricide the Aeschylean Orestes defended what he had done; the Euripidean Orestes calls the killings "murderous / and foul" (E. *El.* 1177–78).

The second minor character, entirely new to the myth, is Electra's farmer husband. Humble though he is, he shows delicacy and self-restraint in respecting Electra's virginity, and he inspires Orestes' disquisition on the unreliability of nobility and wealth as criteria of worth—a recurrent theme of Euripidean drama (see Gregory 2002, pp. 151–59). The Farmer's most important function, however, is to highlight Electra's predicament as a young woman unhappily living out the etymology of her name (*alektros* = "unbedded"). Her marriage-in-name-only places her in an ambiguous position: at the opening of the play the women of the chorus invite her to attend the festival of Hera, but she does not think she can attend—not only because she is in mourning, but also because she belongs neither with the virgins nor with the married women. Electra is painfully conscious that she lives in poverty, yoked to an inferior in what is not even a proper marriage, and conscious, too, of her mother's contrasting enjoyment of her illicit sexual union (E. *El.* 207–12). The ruse of having given birth, by which Electra lures her mother to her death, reflects Electra's preoccupations with sexuality, marriage, and motherhood. This Electra, in contrast to Aeschylus', is vehement rather than strong. Confident that she hates Clytemnestra, she both plans and participates in the matricide, only to discover in the aftermath that her mother was both "loved and unloved" by her children (E. *El.* 1230).

Euripides complicates the character of both Aegisthus and Clytemnestra. Aegisthus is a caricature of a tyrant who stamps on Agamemnon's tomb and plots to kill Electra as well as Orestes. Yet he also shows himself to be conventionally pious and a genial host: he invites Orestes to participate in sacrificing to the local nymphs and places the murder weapon all too trustfully in Orestes' hands, turning himself into the sacrificial victim instead of the priest.

Clytemnestra presents the clearest contrast with her Aeschylean counterpart. Euripides endows her with a number of redeeming qualities. She is powerfully maternal. The Farmer admits that Clytemnestra, "bloodthirsty / as she was, saved [Electra] from Aegisthus' hands" (E. *El.* 27–28). Although she has borne additional children to Aegisthus, she still remembers Iphigenia, the daughter she lost (in *The Libation Bearers,* by contrast, she makes no mention of her). She comes immediately (as Electra predicted) at the news that her daughter has borne a son. Unlike the Aeschylean queen, this Clytemnestra is scrupulous when it comes to religious observance; she is eager to make the proper sacrifices to celebrate the supposed birth. This Clytemnestra not only defends her own conduct (as did her Aeschylean counterpart), but also allows her daughter to speak her mind in rebuttal. She understands and forgives Electra for preferring her father to herself, and confesses that for her own part, "I'm not really / very happy with what I did, dear child" (E. *El.* 1105–6). This milder characterization makes the matricide far more problematic than in Aeschylus, and that, clearly, is Euripides' point.

As the children execute the murder plot the differences from Aeschylus coalesce to produce a very different picture of the matricide and of Apollo, the god who set it in motion. Orestes is able to complete the matricide only by shielding his eyes with his cloak, and no sooner is Clytemnestra dead than her children experience revulsion for what they have done. Like *The Libation Bearers* the tragedy features a *kommos* or ritual lament, but this one follows rather than precedes the murder, and the children grieve for themselves rather than their father. As they relive each traumatic detail of the matricide, Orestes and Electra surprise themselves with their fierce emotions of loss, wrongdoing, and regret. Although Castor's deus ex machina pronouncement promises them eventual security, it also confirms that their sufferings have only just begun: what they face in the immediate future is separation, exile from their native land, persecution by the Furies, and (for Orestes) the ordeal of a homicide trial.

Castor's speech is most significant not for its predictions of the future but for its perspective on the matricide. Castor confirms that (as in Aeschylus) the matricide was ordered by Apollo and demanded by Fate, but in this play the divine authorization does nothing to justify it: "Fate's grim necessity led to what had to be / and the commands of Phoebus, less than wise" (E. *El.* 1301–2; compare 1245–46). If Orestes and Electra are not polluted, it is because Castor holds Apollo, not the two siblings, responsible for the matricide (E. *El.* 1296–97). That these judgments are rendered more in sorrow than in anger by Castor, himself a demigod, lends them added weight. The play ends with a protest against the cruel and obtuse divine commands that have crushed Orestes and Electra. For spectators who remember the Aeschylean vindication of the matricide, this would be a startling and disturbing conclusion.

Sophocles

Arguably the more elaborate the literary treatment of a given motif, the later in the tradition that treatment is likely to occur. Sophocles' *Electra* includes several crescendo effects, suggesting that it is the last of the three Electra plays. First, there is Sophocles' treatment of Agamemnon's funerary rites. In Aeschylus' *The Libation Bearers,* Electra is shut indoors and prevented from mourning her father (*LB* 443–50). In Euripides' *Electra,* more shockingly, Aegisthus is reported to disport himself on the dead king's grave (E. *El.* 326–27). But in Sophocles' *Electra,* Clytemnestra behaves more outrageously still, celebrating the anniversary of his murder with a festival and sacrifices (S. *El.* 278–81). Second, there is Sophocles' treatment of Electra's recognition of Orestes. The Aeschylean Orestes wastes no time disclosing his identity, so the recognition scene occurs at the beginning of *The Libation Bearers.* The Euripidean Orestes delays revealing himself, so the recognition scene occurs toward the middle of Euripides' *Electra.* But in Sophocles' *Electra* the delay is amplified to the point that the recognition of Orestes (which moreover gives rise to a sequel as Orestes reunites Electra with the Tutor) takes place close to the end of the play. As a consequence, Electra as well as Clytemnestra falls victim to the false tale of Orestes' death.

The final crescendo effect is Sophocles' treatment of Clytemnestra's murder. Since Greek tragedy normally avoids enacting death on stage, in all three versions Clytemnestra dies inside the *skēnē.* Aeschylus' Clytemnestra meets her death in silence while the chorus sings that justice has come "at long last" (*LB* 935). Euripides' Clytemnestra is allotted one terrified exclamation (E. *El.* 1167). But Sophocles' Clytemnestra "is given five separate cries . . . express[ing] her isolation . . . , her moving appeal to her son . . . , and her final screams of pain" (Finglass 2007, p. 510). When we add to this evidence Sophocles' apparent rejection of the matricide-as-dilemma approach adopted by Aeschylus and Euripides, and his apparent reversion to the Homeric portrayal of the vengeance as a source of glory, there seems a cogent case to be made in favor of

Sophocles' *Electra* as the last of the three plays (for the advantages of agnosticism on this issue see, however, Finglass 2007, pp. 2–4).

The great problem of Sophocles' *Electra* is that it does not seem to regard the matricide as a problem. This has given rise to two sharply divergent schools of interpretation. One regards the play as a straightforward endorsement of Orestes' revenge reflecting, however puzzlingly, Sophocles' considered view of kin-killing. The other sees the play as suffused with irony: on this reading, Sophocles intends to condemn the matricide, and everything that appears to affirm it must accordingly be taken in the opposite sense (for a review of the two positions see MacLeod 2001, pp. 4–20). Neither perspective does justice to Sophocles' tragedy. In my view, the dramatist does indeed downplay the moral complexities of the vengeance—not because he does not regard matricide as problematic, but because that vein had been so thoroughly mined by Aeschylus and Euripides. Sophocles' treatment shifts the moral ambiguity previously associated with the matricide to a different aspect of the action and opens up perspectives on the myth unexplored by the other dramatists.

That Sophocles minimizes the matricide cannot be denied. His Atreids are not haunted by a family curse, and his Orestes is subject to none of the doubts and hesitations that beset the Aeschylean and, even more conspicuously, the Euripidean Orestes. Brought up in exile, Orestes has been trained for a single purpose, to avenge his father (S. *El.* 11–15, 603–5). When he consulted the oracle at Delphi his question was not whether but how he should carry out the vengeance (S. *El.* 32–34). Since the political dimension of his mission is unproblematic, Sophocles keeps it prominently in view. His Clytemnestra dreams not of past crime or future punishment as in Stesichorus and Aeschylus, but of the reinvigoration of Agamemnon's dynasty: she dreams that Agamemnon's scepter, planted at the family hearth, puts forth "a vigorous young branch that cast its shade / over all the land of Mycenae" (S. *El.* 422–23). Agamemnon's signet ring, the token that ultimately reveals Orestes to his sister, conveys the same dynastic message: as Agamemnon's heir Orestes will restore the political order.

It becomes easier for the spectators to regard the matricide with composure if the victim is portrayed as unsympathetically as is Sophocles' Clytemnestra. It is not enough that she celebrates the anniversary of Agamemnon's death (S. *El.* 278–81). Clytemnestra also berates Electra for saving her brother (S. *El.* 294–98), dresses

Electra in rags (S. *El.* 191), beats and starves her (S. *El.* 1196), and makes plans to lock her away in a dungeon (S. *El.* 380–83). Although she claims to have murdered her husband on account of Iphigenia, the chorus has already identified lust as her driving force (S. *El.* 197). (In contrast to other versions, moreover, Agamemnon is here partially exculpated for Iphigenia's death: Electra's narrative of the events at Aulis makes it clear that Agamemnon had no choice but to sacrifice his daughter, for there was no returning home and no sailing to Troy [S. *El.* 574].) Clytemnestra describes Orestes, spirited from home as a child in order to save his life, as a voluntary exile who "tore himself from my breasts and the care I gave him, / ran away, and became a foreigner" (S. *El.* 776–77)—a brazen example of blaming the victim. This Clytemnestra, in short, is loathsome enough to forfeit audience sympathy.

Loathsome as she is, the matricide is still a shocking act. But Sophocles orders the murders so that Clytemnestra is killed first and Aegisthus second; arguably this reversal from the other dramatists' treatments takes the spotlight off her murder. In contrast to Aeschylus' and Euripides' versions, no Furies arrive in the aftermath. It is true that in the last moments of the play Aegisthus alludes to the family's present and future evils (S. *El.* 1497–98), but his references are too vague and he himself too despicable for his words to carry much weight.

Sophocles' adaptations of the literary tradition support his presentation of the matricide. He revives the concept, not part of the myth since Homer, of the vengeance as a source of glory. Orestes is confident that his fictitious death will make him "safe—and famous" (S. *El.* 60). When Electra attempts to enlist Chrysóthemis as her ally, she describes the public acclaim and enduring reputation that will accrue to them both if they kill the usurpers (S. *El.* 975–86). Sounding the dynastic theme once again, she extols her sister and herself in terms that suggest tyrant-killers more than matricides (Finglass 2007, p. 404).

Sophocles draws on Stesichorus, Aeschylus, and probably Euripides for his damning characterization of Clytemnestra. As in Stesichorus, Clytemnestra has plotted against Orestes' life. As in Stesichorus and Aeschylus, she is haunted by an ominous dream. As in Aeschylus, there is a contrast between her ambivalent reception of Orestes' reported death and the genuine despair of another woman belonging to the household. In Aeschylus the other woman is the nurse; in Sophocles it is Electra, who served as caregiver for her little brother when she was a girl (S. *El.* 1144–48). As in Euripides, finally, the audience hears a good deal from Electra about Clytemnestra's scandalous union with Aegisthus (S. *El.* 98–100, 274–77, 587–88). In Euripides this motif tends (since his Clytemnestra is relatively sympathetic) to direct attention to Electra's own sexually liminal state. In Sophocles, by contrast, it reinforces the awfulness of Clytemnestra.

Aeschylus' *Libation Bearers* provided Sophocles with the germ of a deception plot audacious enough to distract the spectators from the morality of the matricide. In both plays Orestes and Pylades exploit a false report of Orestes' death to gain entry to the palace, but Sophocles expands Aeschylus' brief announcement ("Orestes is dead," *LB* 681) into a prolonged, vivid, and circumstantial account of the chariot race that led to the young man's fatal accident. *The Libation Bearers* contains one fleeting reference to Orestes' ashes, "now encased in a bronze urn" (*LB* 687). In Sophocles, the urn assumes tangible form as a memorable stage prop: Electra cradles it in her arms as she says farewell to her brother, refusing to give it up even as Orestes tries to convince her that he is alive and well.

Borrowings notwithstanding, *Electra* is an eminently Sophoclean play. Like six of Sophocles' seven extant tragedies it features a resolute, independent protagonist who dominates all the characters around her. Sophoclean heroes and heroines are characteristically intelligent and self-aware, and Electra is no exception. In contrast to Orestes, who never knew his mother, she knows Clytemnestra all too well, having lived with her for years in an intimacy that is hateful to them both. She considers her "more tyrant than mother" (S. *El.* 598), and has adopted as her only possible means of resistance a prolonged, public program of lamentation for Agamemnon: "ceaseless, raucous mourning for my poor father" (S. *El.* 133). The women of the chorus rebuke Electra for her behavior, which is both futile and contrary to standards of female decorum; Clytemnestra reviles her for it; Chrysóthemis considers it "silly" (S. *El.* 331). Electra, however, refuses to abandon a course she recognizes as shameful (S. *El.* 254–57, 616–21) but also considers necessary. In her own view she has no choice: "I have to be dreadful in dreadful times" (S. *El.* 221). Sophocles hereby displaces the ambiguity of the matricide onto Electra's policy of ceaseless mourning. As a form of resistance that substitutes words for deeds, her program directs attention to a powerful organizing motif of the play.

The antithesis of language versus action, or word (*logos*) versus deed (*ergon*), is fundamental to Greek thought. Words offer those without power the means to compensate for their inability to act; not surprisingly, they are often associated with women, whereas deeds are associated with men. So it is with Orestes and Electra. Each has a different understanding of the relationship between words and deeds, and each refines that understanding in the course of the play.

Orestes, the man of action, considers words simply a means to an end. In the opening scene he sketches out the scheme whereby he will be dead in report but not in fact: "How could this hurt me? I'll be dead, according to what I say, / but what I do will make me safe—and famous" (S. *El.* 59–60). He is right that the false report will do him no harm; what he does not realize is how much harm it will do his sister, who is almost destroyed by the fiction of his death. Orestes underestimates the power of language; only when he hears Electra's anguished farewell to his (supposed) ashes does he realize the damage his words have caused.

Words are Electra's only weapon against the usurpers, and her policy of mourning her father loudly, persistently, and defiantly moves language as far as it can go in the direction of action. Because she regards her own words as tantamount to deeds, it does not occur to her that some stories may lack a crucial underpinning of fact; won over by the Tutor's vivid account of the chariot race, she fails to consider that his tale might not be true. When her sister Chrysóthemis (a character who is mentioned in Homer, *Iliad* 9.145, but who does not figure in the versions of Aeschylus or Euripides) brings news of the offerings she has seen on Agamemnon's tomb, Electra rejects Chrysóthemis' accurate deduction that Orestes has returned; she puts faith in a stranger's unsupported tale rather than in her sister's trustworthy eyewitness account. In the recognition scene Electra displays the same predisposition: having been assured that the urn contains Orestes' ashes, she has trouble accepting that her brother is alive and stands before her in the flesh.

The messenger speech delivered by the Tutor is designed to deceive, and it succeeds. It also serves, however, as an accurate touchstone of the listeners' dispositions. If Clytemnestra's initial reaction to Orestes' purported death is equivocal, she soon manifests undisguised relief (S. *El.* 773–83). As for Electra, the report of her brother's death spurs her, at long last, to action. Believing that she can no longer rely on Orestes to take action on her behalf, she chooses deeds over words and resolves to kill the usurpers herself.

Although the discovery that Orestes is alive obviates the need for Electra to take independent action, she does not lose sight of her new understanding of the distinction between deeds and words. When her brother urges her to dispense with "too much talk" (S. *El.* 1288), she is able to check her flow of language. Standing guard outside the *skēnē* while Orestes kills their mother within, Electra puts her own terse words at the service of his deed: "Hit her again! Make it twice if you're strong enough" (S. *El.* 1415). In her final exchanges with Aegisthus her speech is double-edged but minimalist. "By the end, Electra, without ceasing to be herself, and without losing her affinity to *logos,* can join effectively in the *ergon* of vengeance" (Woodard 1965, p. 196).

Not everyone will applaud Electra's transformation into a woman of action or countenance her zeal for matricide. Electra has clearly been coarsened by her long ordeal, and the evidence of her implacable anger, together with Sophocles' curious decision to end the play with Aegisthus still alive, has struck some critics (for example, Lloyd 2005, pp. 114–15) as undercutting the ending and leaving the spectators with a lingering sense of uneasiness and foreboding. The case for an ironic interpretation of the ending is strengthened if (as argued by Finglass 2007, p. 546) all or some of the closing lines were written not by Sophocles but by a later interpolator.

Although the Greek of these lines displays some oddities, I regard the ending as genuine. The chorus' final words are consistent with the rest of the play: disturbing though this conclusion may be for some readers and spectators, Sophocles presents the matricide as more of a solution than a problem. In the last of the three *Electra* plays the house of Atreus is freed—albeit at vast emotional cost—from the burden of the past: "Seed of Atreus, how much you suffered / before you won through to freedom—barely— / but perfectly now, from this beginning" (S. *El.* 1508–10).

Justina Gregory

About the Translations

Aeschylus' *Libation Bearers*

The first reading of my translation of the *Oresteia,* in which my translation of *The Libation Bearers* first appeared, was performed at Columbia University, New York, in 1997 by members of the Aquila Theatre Company. A shortened version of the text was staged at the University of South Carolina in 1998. The text of *The Libation Bearers* is based on the edition of A. Garvie (1986).

My main objective in undertaking the translation was to produce a work that was accessible, performable, and dramatic, yet still faithful to the Greek. For those with little knowledge of Greek drama, I sought to create a translation that transmitted the power, passion, tension, and beauty of the plays in a form that was both immediately understandable and dramatically compelling. I did not attempt to re-create the meter of the Greek, preferring a rendering in English better suited to oral delivery by an actor on stage. I did, however, place sung passages in italics and indicate strophic responsion to give the reader a sense of Aeschylus' all-important dramatic form and structure; I have retained those conventions in this volume.

The Greek texts have come down to us without stage directions. Opinions about stage directions have always been controversial and are bound to remain so. However, I feel strongly that one of my responsibilities as translator of a play has been to make informed decisions about stage movements. I have done this based on the experience of staging Greek drama at both Delphi and Epidaurus and in hundreds of modern performance spaces of all shapes and sizes. One benefit of this staging experience is an appreciation of the profound effects of masked acting for stage movement. The opportunity to work with actors proficient in mask, to use them in rehearsal and performance, and to contribute to a fully masked production of the *Oresteia* at the University of South Carolina has proven invaluable in forming my opinions on this subject.

An understanding of the culture and society for which a play was originally conceived is essential to comprehending the work and, in turn, to the creation of a faithful performance. I have thus included brief notes intended to create a frame of reference for the play without detracting from the flow of the text itself.

Peter Meineck (adapted from Meineck 1998)

Euripides' *Electra*

My aim in turning my hand to translation has been to offer a text close enough to the Greek to be usable by teachers and students who wish to study the play, yet not so foreign to the English language that it would embarrass actors to speak the lines, whether in a theater or classroom. I was moved to think about making translations fifteen or so years ago by the experience of a young director—now a playwright—who at fifteen fell in love with Sophocles' *Antigone* and managed to stage it for three performances in Moscow, Idaho. It was a remarkable achievement. The only fault was with the translation, which, because the director was limited to staging a version that was already in the public domain, was stilted and remote.

A translator, like a director, has to make decisions that preclude other possibilities. In addition to providing minimal stage directions (of which there are none in the Greek) for entrances and exits, I have made some allusions to ancient artifacts (Agamemnon "dedicated the lion's share of foreign spoils" to the gods, 7), others to modern literature (Electra claims "mourning becomes me," 182), others timeless (the Farmer is associated with soil or dirt). Some choices were easy—using "heart" instead of "liver" (688), because liver would be too distracting; others less so, like that between "Hades" and "Hell" (662). Other choices impose my interpretation on the reader: that Electra has no slave, for example. In most cases of this type, I have tried to indicate in the notes that there is room for honest dissent (for example, at 1110).

I chose to have the line numbers of my translation more or less match those of the Greek. The translation itself is based on the Murray (1913) and Diggle (1981) Oxford Classical Texts; the commentaries I used most are those of Paley (1874), Denniston (1939), and Cropp (1988).

I would like to thank Diane Arnson Svarlien and John Quinn, anthology editors at Diotima, for their help with my earlier translations; Hackett's readers for their helpful and humane advice; and my husband Lance Luschnig, who read the translation aloud with me and saved it from some unspeakable lines.

My translation of Euripides' *Electra,* first published in this volume, is dedicated to my heroic brother, John Eaton, who died suddenly while I was working on it. χαῖρε, σύγγονε φίλτατε.

Cecelia Eaton Luschnig

Sophocles' *Electra*

Sophocles wrote this play for the stage and I have translated it with the stage in mind, though I have also tried to maintain a high standard of accuracy. At the same time, I have aimed to preserve the choral passages and longer speeches without observing a strict meter or rhyme scheme. Sophocles' poetry is concise, alliterative, and of staggering emotional power, and these qualities tend to be lost in metrical or rhyming translations. Bringing *Electra* into modern idiom took me five years, because it was such an emotionally draining experience that I could not keep it up for long periods—so intense are the anger and grief that animate the play.

On the art of translation, see Woodruff 2005. I have followed the Oxford Classical Text (Lloyd-Jones and Wilson 1990b) except where indicated in the notes. My line numbers follow those of the Greek text as closely as possible.

Readers should understand that the manuscripts contained no stage directions. I have provided stage directions where appropriate, basing them on Peter Meineck's understanding of ancient staging techniques. For the notes, I am often indebted to the commentaries cited. In all things I am indebted to Jebb's brilliant edition (1894) and the commentary to the entire body of Sophocles' work. Finglass (2007) was not available at the time this translation was prepared.

Paul Woodruff (adapted from Meineck and Woodruff 2007)

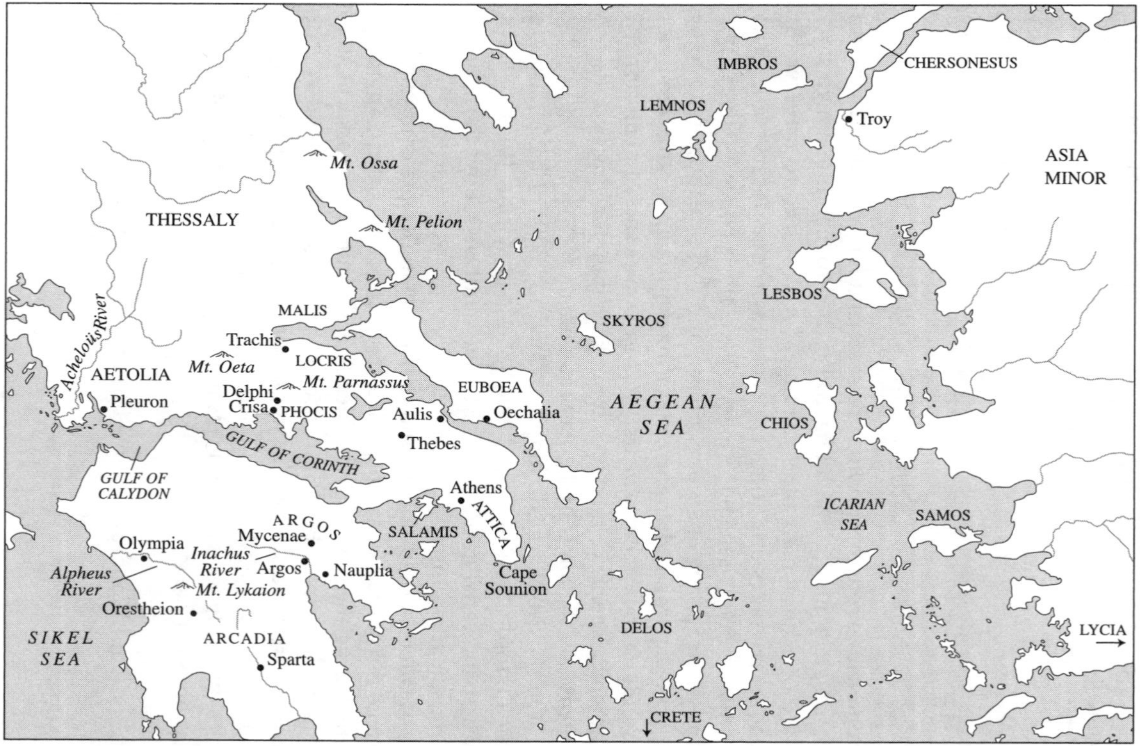

Greece in the Mycenaean Era

House of Pelops Family Tree According to Homer

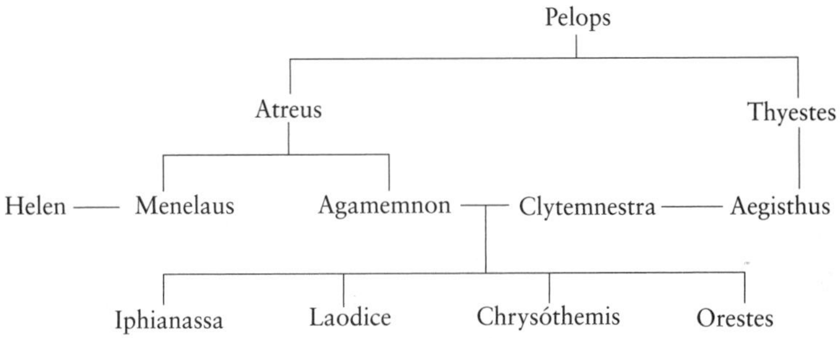

The Electra plays of Aeschylus, Euripides, and Sophocles each draw upon a genealogy for the house of Pelops largely consistent with the one articulated in Homer, with one major exception: according to the playwrights, Agamemnon and Clytemnestra had a daughter named Electra, but the name Electra never occurs in Homer. Instead, Homer gives Agamemnon and Clytemnestra three daughters: Chrysóthemis, Iphianassa, and Laodice. Iphianassa is sometimes identified with Iphigenia, and Laodice may be Homer's name for Electra. Of the three playwrights, only Sophocles mentions Chrysóthemis.

AESCHYLUS

The Libation Bearers

Translated with Notes by Peter Meineck

Cast of Characters

ORESTES	son of Agamemnon and Clytemnestra
PYLADES	his friend, son of Strophius of Phocis
ELECTRA	Orestes' sister
CHORUS	of Eastern slave women
DOORMAN	for the household of Aegisthus
CLYTEMNESTRA	queen of Argos
CILISSA	Orestes' old nurse
AEGISTHUS	ruler of Argos
SERVANT	to Aegisthus and Clytemnestra

The Libation Bearers

SCENE 1: *The tomb of Agamemnon in Argos, seven years after the killing of Agamemnon by Clytemnestra.*

(Enter Orestes and Pylades from the stage left wing into the orchestra)

ORESTES:

Hermes of the Underworld, guardian of my father's power,
be my savior, stand with me in the pursuit of my claim.
I have returned to my land, I have come home.
Father, I call on you, here at your tomb,
hear me, father! Heed my words!
To River Inachus, my nurturer, I offer a lock of hair,
and I lay another here as a mark of my grief.
I was not here, father, to mourn your cruel death,
I could not pay you homage as you lay on the bier.

(Enter the chorus of black-robed slave women from the stage right wing into the orchestra)

Look! There, do you see? A band of black-clad
women making their way toward us?
What does this mean?
More misery for the House?

(The chorus draws nearer to the tomb.)

No, I think they are bringing libations for my father,
to soothe his sprit beneath this earth.
Yes, I am sure of it, look there! I can see Electra,
my sister. She is with them, marked by her grief.
Zeus! Give me revenge for the death of my father!

Tomb of Agamemnon: The orchestra altar may well have served as Agamemnon's tomb.

1: Hermes—the son of Zeus and Maia, invoked in his guise as escort of the dead and spiritual guide.

6: Inachus—the main river of the city and the land of Argos (see map).

Be my ally, and fight at my side!
Pylades, let's hide. We'll keep clear and discover
why these women make this supplication.

(Orestes and Pylades move toward the stage.)

[Strophe 1]

CHORUS:
Sent from the House to bear libations,
heavy hands, beating hard.
Cheeks marked with crimson, gashed,
nails plough furrows, fresh and deep.
For all this life my heart has fed
on tortured cries of grief,
sorrow sounds the tearing
of threadbare fabrics,
sullen folds clothe the breast
that nurture our despair.

[Antistrophe 1]

A hair-raising scream, a fierce
sleep-breathing cry from the prophet,
a shriek in the dead of night.
Terror swept the halls of the House
and fell hard upon the women's rooms.
And the dream diviners,
pledged by the gods to know,
blamed the wrath from those below,
and told of the malice
the killers had stirred.

[Strophe 2]

O Gaia! Earth-Mother!
This is an empty gesture to ward off evil.

21: "These women"—Large funeral processions with hired professional mourners had been a feature of Athenian death rites among the aristocracy. However, at some point in the late sixth or early fifth century, legislation was passed limiting the scale and excessiveness of these ceremonies.

44: Gaia—one of the earliest divinities, nurturer of life, recipient of the dead, and the daughter of Chaos.

That godless woman sends me here,
I fear to let her words be heard.
What can redeem blood once spilled?
Oh miserable hearth!
Oh destructive House!
There is no sun, only hateful gloom,
desolate darkness envelops the House,
where a master was brutally killed.

[Antistrophe 2]

The unconquerable majesty, untamed, invincible,
that once filled the hearts and minds of the people,
is gone now, cast aside—
instead there is only fear.
Happiness is a god, even more than a god,
but the scales of Justice tilt suddenly,
for those who bask in the light,
for those who dwell in the shadows,
for the powerless shrouded by the night.

[Strophe 3]

Nurturing Earth has drunk too much blood,
the gore of vengeance congeals, it will not drain away.
Agonizing ruin infects the guilty,
sickened by devastating suffering.

[Antistrophe 3]

Nothing can remedy the virgin's defilement,
not even all the rivers of the earth, flowing
together in one great torrent, could cleanse
the stain of murder from tainted, bloody hands.

[Epode]

The gods forced their fate on my city.
Destiny took me, from the home of my father,
to lead this life of slavery.

77: "Life of slavery"—The chorus are slaves, possibly captive Trojan women, certainly hailing from the East.

The just and the unjust I must abide,
and force my will to master
the bitter hatred in my mind.
I shed tears behind a veil,
for the unnatural end of my master.
My blood creeps cold with secret grief.

ELECTRA:

Servant women, keepers of the House,
my escort in these rites of atonement,
now I need your advice.
When I pour these burial offerings, what should I say?
What would be right? How can I pray to my father?
Should I say I bring dedications from a loving wife
to her beloved husband, when they come from my mother?
Or should I recite the customary saying:
"Repay those who send these honors,"
for they deserve a gift that matches their evil.
Should I pour them away in silence and disgrace,
just as my father died, and let the earth drink them dry?
Or should I throw this vase behind me, just discard it,
then avert my eyes and just walk away?
I do not have the courage! What should I say
as I pour these liquids on my father's tomb?
Give me your counsel, dear sisters, we share
a bond of common hatred in this house, open your hearts,
don't conceal your thoughts, you need have no fear.
Destiny's day draws near
for both the free and the slave,
tell me if you know a better way.

CHORUS:

Your father's tomb is like an altar to me,
as you have asked, I will speak my mind.

ELECTRA:

Then speak out of respect for my father's grave.

CHORUS:

As you pour, praise those who are loyal.

ELECTRA:

Which of my friends can be called that?

CHORUS:
First, yourself, and then all those who hate Aegisthus.

ELECTRA:
Then I should say this prayer for me, and for you?

CHORUS:
That is for to you to decide, you must learn the answer.

ELECTRA:
Who else can I place on our side?

CHORUS:
Remember Orestes, even though he is far away.

ELECTRA:
A good thought, you were right to remind me.

CHORUS:
Then be mindful of those guilty of murder.

ELECTRA:
What should I say? Teach me, show me the right way.

CHORUS:
Pray that some spirit or a man may one day come.

ELECTRA:
Do you mean to judge or to exact justice?

CHORUS:
Simply state one to kill those who killed.

ELECTRA:
But is it right to ask this of the gods?

CHORUS:
How could it not be right to repay your enemy, evil for evil?

ELECTRA:
Mighty herald of above and below, [165]
Hermes of the Underworld, summon me
the spirits from beneath the earth,
let the sentinels of my father's House hear me.

123: The manuscript places this line at 165, but most scholars place it here.

Call the Earth-Mother who gives all things life,
grows them strong, then receives again their harvest.
As I pour this holy water for the dead,
I call to my father: take pity on me, bring back
dear Orestes, rekindle the light of this House.
Now we live no better than refugees,
sold by our mother in exchange for a man,
Aegisthus, her partner in your murder.
I live like a slave, and Orestes is banished
from his inheritance, while they revel
in the luxurious fruits of your labors.
May the turn of fortune bring Orestes home!
This is my prayer, hear me, father,
grant me the discretion my mother lacks,
keep my hands clean and pure.
These prayers are for us, for our enemies I say:
bring the avenger into the light,
let Justice kill the killers!
In the midst of my prayers for good,
I say for them a prayer for evil.
Send us your blessings, send them up high,
let gods, Earth and Justice bring victory!
These are my prayers as I pour this libation.
Sound the death cry to flower my prayers,
sing the invocation in honor of the dead!

(Electra pours the libation.)

CHORUS:
Let the tears splash, falling,
for a fallen master,
splashing this bastion to evil.
We pour these libations
to avert the pollution.
Hear me, hear me, royal master,
your spirit gripped by darkness.

Otototototototo!
Let him come, a man of the spear,

142–51: Electra, guided by the servant women, turns an offering contrived by Clytemnestra to appease the dead into a call for vengeance.

a liberator of the House,
his Scythian bow bent back,
Ares' death-bolts ready,
he closes in, sword in hand.

ELECTRA:
The earth has drunk the libations poured for my father.

(Electra sees the lock of hair on the tomb.)

But wait! There is something new, here.

CHORUS:
Tell me, my heart throbs with foreboding.

ELECTRA:
Someone has laid a lock of hair on the tomb.

CHORUS:
Does it come from a man or a young girl?

ELECTRA:
That is easy, anyone could guess.

CHORUS:
How? The youth must teach her elders.

ELECTRA:
I am the only one who could have cut this lock.

CHORUS:
Yes, those that should mourn, can only hate.

ELECTRA:
And yet it looks very much like . . .

CHORUS:
Like what? Tell me.

ELECTRA:
Like my hair, it looks exactly like mine.

CHORUS:
Could it be a secret offering from Orestes?

162: Scythia was the name used for the region spreading from the Danube to the Caucasus. The area provided archers for Athenian forces in the sixth century. The bow may have been regarded primarily as a weapon associated with hunting and the young male initiate.

ELECTRA:
It does look like his hair.

CHORUS:
But how could he dare to come here?

ELECTRA:
He has sent this lock of hair to honor his father.

CHORUS:
Then we have all the more reason for tears:
this means he will never again set foot in this land.

ELECTRA:
A sickening wave surges over me,
an arrow strikes and pierces my heart,
my eyes shed torrents of thirsty tears,
falling relentlessly like a winter storm.
And as I gaze at this lock, how could I imagine
that any other could claim title to this?
The killer could not have cut it,
my mother, who turned her profane mind
against her own children, against her very name.
But how can I accept that this offering
could have come from my dear Orestes?
Oh! Hope is fawning on me.
If only hope had the clear voice of a herald,
then my whirling mind would not be torn in two.
I would know for sure that this lock was severed
from the head of an enemy and I should cast it out,
or that it came from a kinsman, laid in sympathy,
adorning this tomb in honor of my father.
We call on the gods; they know the storms
that send us spinning like sailors on the high seas,
and if by some happy fate we are delivered,
even the smallest sapling can grow into a mighty tree.

(Electra sees footprints on the ground.)

Another sign! Look at these tracks,
a pair of footprints, they are like mine.
There are two sets of marks here, his own,
and these must be his companion's.
Look at the marks left by the heel and the sole,

they are the same as mine, the same size . . .
This is agony! All reason is destroyed!

(Orestes moves toward the altar and presents himself to Electra.)

ORESTES:
Your prayer has been fulfilled, proclaim it to the gods
and pray for the future, praise your good fortune.

ELECTRA:
Why? What has divine grace ever given me?

ORESTES:
You see the sight you have prayed for.

ELECTRA:
How can you know my prayers?

ORESTES:
I know about Orestes and how he fills your heart.

ELECTRA:
But how have my prayers been answered?

ORESTES:
Here I am, I am your nearest, your dearest.

ELECTRA:
This is a trick, and you are a stranger trying to trap me in your net.

ORESTES:
Then I am plotting against myself.

ELECTRA:
Are you mocking me in my misery?

ORESTES:
If I mock your misery, then I mock mine.

ELECTRA:
Then, should I call you—are you really—Orestes?

ORESTES:
You still do not realize though you see me yourself,
yet, when you saw the lock I had cut in mourning,

and were following the tracks of my steps,
your heart raced at the thought of seeing me.
Take the lock and hold it next to the place it came from.
You see? It is your brother's, the same as yours.

(He shows her a small piece of woven fabric.)

Look at this weaving, the work of your hand,
the strokes of your shuttle, the animal motif.

(Electra begins to react joyously.)

Control yourself! Don't loose your mind for joy.
Our closest kin are both our cruelest foes.

ELECTRA:
You are the closest and dearest to your father's House.
How I wept for you, the seed of hope, salvation!
Be bold, be strong, win back the House of your father!
Bright-eyed joy! Four loves in one for me.
It is right to give you the name of our father,
and the love I should have felt for mother,
I turn to you, for I most justly hate her.
Yours is the love for my sister, savagely sacrificed,
and as my faithful brother you paid me honor.
Let Power, Justice, and Zeus the Third,
mightiest of them all, stand at your side.

ORESTES:
Zeus! Zeus! Behold our cause!
Look on the brood bereft of their eagle sire,
who died entwined in the coils of a vicious viper.
Look on the starving orphans, ravaged by hunger,
too young to carry their father's prey to shelter.
Here you see Electra and Orestes,
children robbed of their father,
both outcasts, exiled from our own House.
Our father sacrificed and paid you great honor.
If you destroy his nestlings who will serve
your lavish banquets, as he once did?

232: The nature of this weaving is uncertain from the text. Perhaps it is something like a family crest.

If you destroy the eagle's brood,
man will never again believe your signs.
If the royal tree withers and dies,
your altars will be ignored
on the day the bulls are sacrificed.
You can rebuild the House to former glory,
raise and restore it from a pile of ruins.

CHORUS:
Speak softly, son and daughter, saviors
of your father's hearth, you may be overheard,
rumors can be spread and reach the ears
of those in power. I wish them dead,
and to see their blood boiling in the flames.

ORESTES:
The great oracle of Apollo will never betray me,
it is his mandate that I should endure this trial.
His shrill prophecies wrenched my guts and chilled
me to the bone, they foretold storms of suffering
if I did not avenge my father's killers.
He said to kill the way they killed,
and claim my birthright like a savage bull,
or pay the penalty myself with a life
gripped by evil, and full of pain.
He revealed to me the malicious rancor
that festers below and infects mankind,
the malignant sores that thrive on flesh,
their scurvy jaws devouring the natural health,
pallid fur sprouting from the putrid pus.
He told of the onslaught by the avenging Furies
the progeny of a father's spilled blood.
How, from the darkest depths, the death-bolt
would pierce, as the murdered kin beg for revenge.
Insanity and paranoia would haunt the night,
visions of scowling faces peering from the gloom,
tormented and deranged, driven from cities,
a body battered by the brazen scourge.
The cup of fellowship can never be shared,
and the thank-offering cannot be poured.
Dragged from altars by a father's unseen wrath,
none can offer shelter, there can be no sanctuary,

just a lonely death, disgraced and despised,
wasting away, reduced to nothing.
These then were the oracles, how could I not act on them?
Even if I did not, the deed must still be done,
I have many motives of my own that drive me:
the god's command, the great sorrow I feel for my father,
and the burden of my stolen birthright.
And what of my people, the finest of men,
who conquered Troy with their sterling spirit?
They should not be ruled by a pair of women!
Yes, he's a woman at heart, we'll soon see that for ourselves.

CHORUS:
Mighty Destinies come,
fulfill the will of Zeus,
Justice veer the course,
words of hate fulfill hateful
words. Justice screams
and demands her price.
Bloody blow pays bloody
blow. "The doer suffers,"
sounds the saying, three times old.

[Strophe 1]

ORESTES:
Oh father, sad father!
What to say, what to do,
to soar your distant spirit
from the death bed's tight
embrace? Can light transcend
the darkness? This lament
will grace you with some honor,
son of Atreus, lying here.

[Strophe 2]

CHORUS:
Child, the ravenous jaws of fire
can never quell the spirit dead,
in time the rage will surely flare.
Our death-rattle batters

to make the harm appear,
to rouse your father, your creator.
All wail the vendetta song,
that stirs, and seeks the sin.

[Antistrophe 1]

ELECTRA:
Now father, hear my grief,
I add my voice, my tears.
Two children at your tomb
to chant the dirge of death.
Receive at your grave
the exile and the suppliant.
What is good? What is evil?
Can we ever conquer Ruin?

[Epode]

CHORUS:
But if the gods desire, we may yet
sing a sweeter sounding strain.
Not death-wails beside the tomb,
for the song of invocation will fill the halls of kings,
filling the loving cup to toast the restitution.

[Strophe 3]

ORESTES:
If only at Troy,
Father, a Lycian spear
had cut you down.
Your legacy would glorify the House,
and the name of your children
would be met with respect.
Your tomb would stand high
in a land across the sea,
no burden for this House to bear.

346: Lycia was a region in southwestern Asia Minor (see map). The Lycians were allies of the Trojans and were led by Sarpedon.

[Antistrophe 2]

CHORUS:
He'd be welcomed by comrades,
his men who fell with honor.
He'd be first beneath the earth,
a majestic, stately prince,
a minister for the mighty,
who rule the realm below.
He was a king while he lived,
his authority the Destinies ordained,
the sovereign scepter was his to hold.

[Antistrophe 3]

ELECTRA:
No, never at Troy,
father, death beneath the walls,
lying beside the war-dead,
buried by Scamander's straits.
I wish instead, your killers
had died your despicable death,
then in every place the people
would learn of their fate,
and this pain we'd never know.

[Epode]

CHORUS:
Child, your dreams gleam brighter than gold,
a treasured fortune, beyond the northern winds.
You have the power to speak of great things,
but the crack of the double lash stings deep.
We have our allies beneath the earth,
though power is held by those we hate,
their hands are tainted, they are unclean.
It is you, the children, who will seize the day!

373: "Beyond the northern winds"—where lay the land of the Hyperboreans, a legendary people who were said to lead perfect lives.

[Strophe 4]

ORESTES:
That strikes the ear,
piercing like an arrow.
Zeus, Zeus, force vengeance
up from below, rain down Ruin
on depraved and defiant hands.
Fulfill the debt we owe the parents.

[Strophe 5]

CHORUS:
Let me be first to yell
the hallowed call, flaring up
as the man is struck
and the woman dies.
Should I hide what's deep inside,
hovering in my mind? Bitter
blasts rage before my heart,
my savage soul seethes with spite.

[Antistrophe 4]

ELECTRA:
And when will Zeus
clench his fist and strike them?
Yes, yes, shatter their skulls!
Restore this land's faith.
I want Justice from injustice.
Hear me earth, and powers below.

CHORUS:
It is the law, that spilled blood soaking
the ground demands blood in return.
Murder screams for the Furies
to stand for those long dead,
to bring on Ruin in the trail of Ruin.

[Strophe 6]

ORESTES:
Oh you infernal powers!
Look you curses of the dead!

Look at the last of Atreus,
helpless, homeless, and shamed.
Which way to turn? Help me, Zeus!

[Antistrophe 5]

CHORUS:
My heart shudders
to hear this despair,
I lose all hope,
it repels my blood
darkening within.
But the pain relents,
as new hope dawns
in all her radiant beauty.

[Antistrophe 6]

ELECTRA:
What should our prayers be saying,
that we suffer the pain of our parents?
She tries to fawn, we'll not be charmed,
like savage wolves, we'll not be tamed,
no mother comfort soothes our rage.

[Strophe 7]

CHORUS:
We beat the Persian death-wail,
the way of the Cissian wailing-woman,
clenched fists splattering blood,
hands stretching higher, reaching,
smashing, crashing, the blows rushing,
pounding against my wretched head.

[Strophe 8]

ELECTRA:
Oh cruel, shameless mother,
bitter bier that bore him.

424: Cissia was an area of Persia surrounding the city of Susa in what is now southwestern Iran. Excessive displays of mourning were associated with the East.

The king denied to his people,
the man denied his wake.
How could she bury him unmourned!

[Strophe 9]

ORESTES:
He was humiliated and disgraced,
but she will pay for my father,
by the will of the spirit,
by the will of these hands.
I will do away with her, then I can die.

[Antistrophe 9]

CHORUS:
He was mutilated of manhood,
and she buried him like this,
to ensure that his death
would be too hard to bear.
Know the dishonor done to your father.

[Antistrophe 7]

ELECTRA:
You speak of my father's death,
but I was shut away, worthless,
confined to chambers like a dog.
Laughter died and how I wept,
secret tears of forbidden grief.
Hear me! Carve it on your mind.

[Antistrophe 8]

CHORUS:
Let this prick your conscience—
keep a fixed mind, be strong.
It stands just as it stands,

439: "Mutilated of manhood"—The practice of *maschalismos* involved cutting off the genitalia of a murder victim and hanging them under the armpits before burial. This was a method of rendering the corpse powerless to avenge itself.

You burn to know the rest.
Steel your hearts and go with Rage.

[Strophe 10]

ORESTES:
I call you father, stand with your kin.

ELECTRA:
Through the tears I ask this of you.

CHORUS:
We come together, we echo the call.
Hear us! Come into the light!
Stand with us against the hated!

[Antistrophe 10]

ORESTES:
Force meet force, right meet right!

ELECTRA:
Gods, fulfill our rights with justice!

CHORUS:
I shudder to hear these prayers.
Doom's day has long been waiting.
Let it come, let the prayers be answered!

[Strophe 11]

The agony of generations.
The blood-soaked blow.
The pandemonium of Ruin.
The cruel, insufferable grief,
such unrelenting pain.

[Antistrophe 11]

The House can be healed,
but not from outside,
the cure is found within,
savage, brutal bloodshed.
Gods below, this is your hymn!

[Epode]

Hear us, blessed powers of the earth,
answer our prayers, send us your help,
guide your children to their victory!

ORESTES:
Father, you were denied a kingly death.
Hear me! Give me power over the House.

ELECTRA:
Father, help me, help me destroy
Aegisthus, help to set me free!

ORESTES:
Then your rightful feast-day can be founded,
or else the savory flesh charred for the earth
will starve you of honor while feeding the dead.

ELECTRA:
And I will pour my dowry out to you,
I'll bring wedding wine from my father's store,
first and foremost to revere your tomb.

ORESTES:
O Earth, raise my father to watch my fight!

ELECTRA:
O Persephone, give us your beautiful power!

ORESTES:
Remember the bath, that bathed you in blood.

486: "My dowry"—Under Athenian marital custom, a fatherless girl was given in marriage by her nearest male relative. The bride received a dowry from her guardian to help support her new family. Electra recognizes Orestes, not Aegisthus, as her guardian. Therefore, she cannot be married until Orestes reclaims his ancestral house.

490: Persephone—the daughter of Zeus and Demeter and the wife of Hades. She spent half of the year in the Underworld and half with her mother above. She is thus associated with the renewal of the seasons and the restoration of life.

ELECTRA:
Remember the net they devised to trap you.

ORESTES:
Fettered in chains not made of metal.

ELECTRA:
That shameless, deceitful shroud.

ORESTES:
Father, awake and answer this disgrace!

ELECTRA:
Father, dear father, hold up your head!

ORESTES:
Send Justice to fight at our side,
give us the match, hold for hold.
For your defeat we'll throw them down.

ELECTRA:
Hear me, father, one last cry,
look at your fledglings, nestling at your tomb,
pity the male and female, pity your children.

ORESTES:
The House of Pelops must survive;
dead but not dead, your memory lives with us.
The children sustain the dead man's name,
like buoyant corks lining a net,
saving the mesh from sinking to the depths.

ELECTRA:
Hear us! This lament is for you.
Heed our words, save your honor.

CHORUS:
No one could find fault with your words,
this tomb, his fate, they have never been mourned.
Now your minds are set, it is time for action.
You must put the spirit to the test.

ORESTES:
Yes, and I will not stray from this path, but tell me
why she sent these libations? What compelled her,

after so long, to try to soothe this incurable wound?
It is a paltry offering to send the unconscious dead.
What kind of gifts are these? They fall so short
of her crime, what was she thinking?
"Pour everything out for the blood you have shed,
you're wasting your time in appeasing the dead."
Do you know why she did it? Can you explain it?

CHORUS:
I know, my son, I was there: she had terrible dreams,
terror stalked her nights, she shook with fear,
and so that godless woman sent these libations.

ORESTES:
Do you know what the dreams meant, can you tell me?

CHORUS:
She dreamed she gave birth to a snake, she said it herself!

ORESTES:
A snake? What else?

CHORUS:
She laid it down, and wrapped it like a baby.

ORESTES:
What? Did she see this creature feeding?

CHORUS:
She dreamed that she suckled it herself.

ORESTES:
But, a snake? It must have slashed her breast?

CHORUS:
It sucked her milk, clotted with blood.

ORESTES:
It has its meaning, the snake represents a man.

CHORUS:
She screamed in her sleep and woke shaking with fear.
Torches flared up, burning away the blind darkness,
and lamps lit the halls to comfort the mistress.
She sent these libations to appease the dead,
hoping for a cure to cut away her affliction.

ORESTES:

I pray to the earth and to the tomb of my father,
that this dream finds fulfillment in me.
I can see it now, it all falls into place.
The snake came from the same place as I.
She wrapped it in the same cloths that I wore.
It suckled at the breast that nurtured me,
fouling her precious milk with clotted blood,
and this sight made her scream in terror.
As she has raised this gruesome omen,
so she must die. I am the snake,
I will be the one to kill her and fulfill this dream.

CHORUS:

Then you are my prophet, I believe your interpretation.
Let it be as you say. Let your friends play their part.
Tell us what you need us to do.

(Pylades moves toward Orestes and Electra.)

ORESTES:

The plan is simple. My sister must promise
to keep our meeting secret and go back inside.
They used stealth to kill a man of honor,
and so by stealth they will die, trapped
by the same snare. So Apollo has ordained,
and the prophet god has never yet proved wrong.
I will take what I need and dress like a stranger.
This is Pylades, an ally, a friend to our house,
he and I will go together to the gates.
We both know the Parnassian dialect,
so we will sound like men from Phocis.
The doorkeepers may well turn us away,
after all, an evil spirit dwells in that House,
then, we simply wait, so that anyone passing by
the House will assume the worst and say:
"Why does Aegisthus shut his gates to guests?
Is he at home? Does he know these men are here?"
Once in, across the threshold, I'll find him

563: Mt. Parnassus overlooks Delphi and the region of central Greece to the south of Mt. Parnassus known as Phocis (see map).

sitting there on my father's throne.
He'll come to meet me, face to face,
I'll fix his stare and he'll look away,
then before he can say "Where are you from?"
he'll be a corpse, on the end of my swift sword.
The Fury, with its unquenchable thirst for death,
will drain a third cup of thick, pure blood.

Electra, you must keep a close watch in the House
for this plan to be successful and turn out well.
You women, make sure you hold your tongues,
keep silent and speak only when you need to.
For my part, I call on my father here
to steady my sword as I leave for the fight.

(Exit Orestes, Pylades, and Electra through the stage right wing)

[Strophe 1]

CHORUS:
The Earth nurses countless creatures,
hideous fiends, gruesome beasts.
The Sea cradles terrible monsters,
infested waters that poison man.
The Sky is streaked by deadly lights
that break the shackles of heaven.
The bird on the wing and the beast
of the field know well the raging
storm-winds of god-sent wrath.

[Antistrophe 1]

But who can explain men
and their audacious minds?
Or the reckless thoughts of women,
the brazen lust that consummates
the marriage of mortal ruin?
A seduction of loveless lust,
that perverts and overwhelms
both man and beast alike.

[Strophe 2]

Those who hold right minds,
have heard of Althaea,
scheming daughter of Thestius,
and her plots, burned in the flames.
She threw in the fire the bloody torch,
saved from the time the infant first cried.
The life of the torch for the life of the child,
until Destiny marked the day
when life burned away.

[Antistrophe 2]

There is another hateful legend,
the story of Scylla, bloody bitch,
enticed by her enemies with gold
to murder her own dear father.
Lured by the gift of Minos,
a golden necklace from Crete,
she cut the magic lock of Nisus.
He slept and drew his last breath
as Hermes came and took him in death.

[Strophe 3]

As I recount these bitter stories
I remember a loveless marriage,
one that cursed a House.
Plots connived in the mind of a woman,
against the man, the warrior,
against the man, feared by foes.

604: Althaea—the mother of the hero Meleager, who was told by the spirits of Destiny that her son would live only as long as a brand on her fire. Althaea removed the brand and kept it safe until she learned that Meleager had killed his brothers. In a fit of rage, she threw the brand on the fire, destroying her son.

614: Scylla—the daughter of Nisus, the mythical king of Megara, which lay to the west of Attica. Nisus had a purple lock of hair that served to protect his city. King Minos of Crete, an enemy of the Megarians, seduced Scylla. Bribed with a necklace, she cut off the lock of Nisus, which destroyed her father and betrayed her city to its foes.

A House dishonored, a stone-cold hearth,
ruled by a womanly, cowardly spear.

[Antistrophe 3]

The Lemnian story is first among evils,
a hideous tale of abject atrocity.
The name of Lemnos is burned in disgrace,
the title for each new vile crime.
Fouled by the guilt, detested by the gods,
banished from mankind, their strain died out.
No one respects what is despised by gods.
Which of these stories was I wrong to tell?

SCENE 2: *The House of Atreus in Argos.*

(Enter Orestes and Pylades from the stage right wing into the orchestra)

[Strophe 4]

The sword rips through the lungs;
the keen blade, wielded by Justice,
tears down deep. Right has been wronged,
for they overstepped the mark,
respect for Zeus was trampled underfoot.

(Orestes and Pylades mount the stage and approach the doors.)

[Antistrophe 4]

The anvil of Justice is rooted firm,
Destiny has already forged the sword.

629: "A stone-cold hearth"—a reference to the custom in Argos of extinguishing the hearth fire when the head of the family died and of relighting it to mark a new succession.

630: "A womanly, cowardly spear"—a reference to Aegisthus.

631: The Lemnian women murdered their husbands in a fit of jealousy.

638: The exit of Orestes, Pylades, and Electra at 584, the preceding information, and the intervening choral song, followed by the entry of Orestes and Pylades onto the stage, would have been sufficient to mark the scene change from the tomb of Agamemnon to the House of Atreus.

The child is brought home to pay the debt
by the ever scheming, infamous Fury.
The stain of bloodshed will be cleansed.

(Orestes knocks on the doors.)

ORESTES:
Boy! Boy! Can't you hear me knocking at the door?
Is anybody there! Boy! Boy! Is anyone at home?
For the third time, will someone come out,
if Aegisthus welcomes strangers to this house?

(The doorman's voice is heard from within the house.)

DOORMAN:
All right! All right! I can hear you. Who are you and where are you from?

ORESTES:
Tell the heads of this house that I am here,
I have come to see them with fresh news.
Be quick about it! Night's dark chariot
races on, and it is time for the traveler
to put in at a house of hospitality.
Have someone in authority come out,
the mistress in charge, though the man
would be more fitting. Feminine delicacy veils
words in obscurity, man to man, a conversation
is confident, with plain speaking and straight talk.

(Enter Clytemnestra from the doors)

CLYTEMNESTRA:
Strangers, please, your needs are our pleasure,
we have all you would expect from a house
such as this, warm baths and soft beds to soothe
your cares away, and honest eyes to watch your sleep.
If there are other matters, needing more serious consideration,
then that is a task that must be shared between men.

ORESTES:
I am a foreigner, a Daulian from Phocis.
Now at journey's end I can unyoke my feet and rest.

674: Daulis was a city near Delphi in Phocis (see map).

I was on my way, pack and all, to Argos
and I came across a stranger, another traveler.
We told each other where we were going, and as we talked
I learned his name, Strophius the Phocian.
He saw I was Argos bound and asked me to do him justice
by delivering this message: "Orestes is dead."
He stressed that I must be sure to tell his parents
and to inquire whether his family would want him home,
or if he should lie buried in the land where he lived,
an eternal guest, a migrant in a foreign land.
He asked that I convey their wishes back to him.
His remains are now encased in a bronze urn,
and Strophius said that his loss was deeply mourned.
I've told you all I heard, but I should really be speaking
to the head of the house. I must inform his parents.

CLYTEMNESTRA:
Oh! We are besieged by ruin!
Oh damned curse that grips this House!
Nothing escapes your gaze, your deadly bolts
fly so very far, nothing is out of harm's way.
You strip me of my loved ones, plunge me into despair!
And now Orestes, though he had the sense
not to set foot in this swamp of destruction.
Now Hope has gone, the one cure
for these evil, maddening rites.
Condemn Hope as a traitor, Hope has betrayed us!

ORESTES:
I wish that I could have come to know the comforts
of such an affluent house by bringing good news.
Where can we find more kindness than the ties
that bind the guest and host? But to my mind
it would have been a breach of a sacred duty
not to have performed this obligation for a friend.
I gave my word and was bound by the code of hospitality.

679: In *Agamemnon* 859–86, Clytemnestra justifies Orestes' absence from the palace to the newly returned Agamemnon by claiming that upon hearing rumors of Agamemnon's death, she had entrusted Orestes to the care of their ally Strophius of Phocis, out of fear of a rebellion by the people.

CLYTEMNESTRA:
Be assured you will receive no less than you deserve,
nor be any less a friend under the roof of this house.
We would have soon heard the news all the same.
Following the long day's journey, the weary traveler
should rest. It is time you were made at home.
Women, show this man to the guest rooms,
take his traveling companion with him,
let them enjoy the hospitality of this house.
It is your responsibility; they are in your charge.
I will share this news with the head of the house,
and we will consult our many friends,
as we consider this turn of events.

(Exit Orestes, Pylades, and Clytemnestra through the doors)

CHORUS:
Sisters, women of the House,
when will we have the power
to speak out for Orestes?
Sacred earth, sacred mound
that entombs the Sea Lord,
covering the corpse of a king.
Now hear us! Now help us!
Now is the hour of stealthy Persuasion
to come and stand at his side.
Come Hermes, come Night,
guide the work of his deadly sword.

(Enter Cilissa, the nurse, from the doors)

Look there, Orestes' old nurse is coming out, crying.
It seems the stranger is about his vile work.
Where are you going, Cilissa?
Why are you crying?

CILISSA:
The mistress has ordered me to summon Aegisthus
as quickly as I can. He must come and hear the news,
man to man, so it'll be clear. In front of us servants
she was all doom and gloom, but her eyes were smiling
deep down, at what had worked out well for her.

But not for the House, no, it's the curse, I know it,
the news those strangers brought made that clear,
and I'll bet he'll be overjoyed when he finds out.
Oh the misery of it all! All the old pain mixed together,
right here in this House of Atreus, it's too much to bear.
It breaks my heart to think on it.
But this, I've never known agony like this,
I withstood all the other troubles, flushed them out,
but my dear Orestes, I spent my soul on him,
and I raised him when his mother passed him to me.
I never complained, even though his screaming
would keep me up half the night, I worked
my fingers to the bone for him, all for nothing!
A baby's like a little animal, it can't think for itself,
it needs to be nursed. You have to know its mind.
I mean, when he was that small he couldn't talk,
so he couldn't tell me if he was hungry, or thirsty,
or when he wanted to pee, and a baby's insides are a law
unto themselves, let me tell you! I had to foresee
his every need, and a lot of the time I was wrong,
then I would have to wash his little baby clothes.
Washerwoman and child-minder all rolled into one,
I was an expert at both, a real professional,
which is why Orestes' father entrusted him to me.
Now they tell me he is dead and I've suffered it all.
So I have the task of fetching the man who fouled
this House, and see him rejoice to hear this news.

CHORUS:
How did she tell him to come?

CILISSA:
What do you mean? Say that again, I don't understand.

CHORUS:
Will he be bringing his guards or coming alone?

CILISSA:
She said that he should bring his guards.

CHORUS:
No, don't tell the master that, not if you hate him.
Tell him instead to come alone, quickly,

and be cheerful so that he will not be suspicious,
the messenger can make the warped word straight.

CILISSA:
What! Are you happy to have heard this news?

CHORUS:
Why not? Zeus can avert an ill wind.

CILISSA:
How can that be? Orestes is gone, this House has lost all hope.

CHORUS:
Not yet. It would be a poor prophet who predicted that.

CILISSA:
What do you mean, do you know something that I don't?

CHORUS:
Go now, take your message, follow your orders.
The cares of the gods are for the gods to take care of.

CILISSA:
Then I'll go and do what you want
and with the help of the gods may it be for the best!

(Exit Cilissa through the stage right wing)

[Strophe 1]

CHORUS:
Now I pray to you, Zeus,
father of the Olympian gods.
Grant good fortune to the rightful
rulers of the house, who yearn
to see discretion rule.
I call out in the name of Justice,
Zeus protect her, guard her well.

[Mesode 1]

Zeus, Zeus, guide him into the halls,
and set his enemies before him.
If you raise him to greatness
you will be generously repaid,
a double measure, no, a triple reward!

[Antistrophe 1]

You see the young colt of the man you loved;
he is yoked to a chariot of suffering.
Set a measured pace on his course,
sustain his steady stride,
let us see him come around
the final homeward bend.

[Strophe 2]

You inside the House, reveling
in your luxury, do you hear!
Hear me, sympathetic gods,
pay the debt of past bloodshed
with this just, fresh slaughter.
Then may the House be purged
of the murders known of old.

[Mesode 2]

Apollo of the beautiful chasm,
let this man raise his household's head,
let its loving eyes peer out
to gaze upon the light of freedom
from behind the dismal veil.

[Antistrophe 2]

Help us, Hermes,
child of Maia.
He can veer a favoring course,
reveal the unseen,
speak the hidden words.
He can bring to day the dark of night
and dim their eyes with shrouded sight.

807: "The beautiful chasm"—At Delphi, Apollo's seat of prophecy, there was believed to be a deep chasm over which the priestess sat. The power of the Earth rising up from below was said to influence the priestess.

813: Maia—daughter of the Titan Atlas, and one of the Pleiades; Maia means "mother" or "nurturer."

[Strophe 3]

And when the House is set free,
we women will raise our voices,
high and loud, strong and steady,
and sing the blessing of fine, fair winds:
"The ship sets sail and all is well!"
We all will prosper, we'll share the gain,
Ruin will leave us and go far from our friends!

[Mesode 3]

When the time comes for you to act,
be strong. When she cries out, "My child!"
Say, "My father's child!" and do the deed.
You won't be blamed for the course of Ruin.

[Antistrophe 3]

Place the heart of Perseus in your breast,
repay the debt of those you love,
those that lie beneath the earth,
and those who still stand on it.
Go inside against the Gorgon,
loose Ruin on her murderous spree,
behold the guilty, and then destroy.

(Enter Aegisthus from the stage right wing)

AEGISTHUS:
I was told that I should come and hear the news.
Apparently a stranger has arrived with the message,
that Orestes is dead, words I wished we would never
have to hear. How can this House bear another blow
and its murderous, festering wound not drench us in terror?

831: Perseus—a legendary hero who was sent to kill Medusa the Gorgon, a female monster who could turn men to stone. Perseus decapitated Medusa with the help of Athena and Hermes.

835: The myth of Perseus and the Gorgon was closely connected with the initiation rites of young men.

Enter Aegisthus: It may have been that this entrance occurred earlier in the choral song, in order to give the actor playing Aegisthus time to enter the orchestra from the deep wing and even to mount the stage.

How can I tell if this really is the living truth
or just a fearful rumor spread by women,
a spark of fire flaring up that flickers and falls away?
What can you tell me about this?
I want to set my mind at rest.

CHORUS:
We have heard the story, but go inside and hear
the strangers for yourself. The power of a message
can never equal firsthand news from the man himself.

AEGISTHUS:
I want to see this messenger and question him again.
I want to know if he witnessed the death in person,
or if he is repeating some vague rumor he's heard.
I'll not be fooled, my mind sees with sharp eyes.

(Exit Aegisthus through the doors)

CHORUS:
Zeus, Zeus, what should I say?
Where should I begin my prayer?
My intentions are worthy, I ask the gods for help,
but how can I find any fitting words?
Now the bloodstained blades
that cut men down are being raised,
to strike the blow that forever ends
the House of Agamemnon.
Or the son will strike the sparks of freedom's fire,
and claim the throne of this city
to inherit his father's fortune.
The challenger in this final round,
godlike Orestes, one to throw two.
Let Orestes win the victory!

(The chorus hears a cry from behind the doors.)

AEGISTHUS:
Ai! Ai!

CHORUS:
There! There it is!
What is happening, what does this mean for the House?
Keep back, until this terror is over,

we must appear blameless.
The fight is over, and what will be, will be.

(Enter a servant of Aegisthus from the doors)

SERVANT:
No! It is the end! My master has been cut down!
No more, no more, Aegisthus is no more!
Come quickly, help me break down the door
to the women's rooms, we must unbar the bolts,
it takes the strength of a young arm, help me!
It is too late for Aegisthus, he is dead,
but Clytemnestra! Get up! Get up!
I'm wasting my breath, are you asleep in there?
Get up! Don't you hear me, are you deaf to my shouts?
Where is Clytemnestra? What is she doing?
It is her neck on the block now, and Justice is poised to strike.

(Enter Clytemnestra from the doors)

CLYTEMNESTRA:
What ever is the matter? What is all this shouting in the house?

SERVANT:
The living are killed by the dead!

CLYTEMNESTRA:
I know what this riddle means,
we killed by deceit and by deceit we die.
Quickly, bring me the man-killing axe.

(Exit servant through the doors)

Victory or defeat? We have come this far.
Now we will know, once and for all.

(Enter Orestes from the doors)

ORESTES:
You, I want you. He has done his part.

Enter Clytemnestra: It would have proved dramatically effective, as well as practical, for the doors to remain open here until 930.

889: "Man-killing axe"—There was a tradition in art and myth that Clytemnestra killed Agamemnon with a large, double-headed sacrificial axe.

CLYTEMNESTRA:
No! My dear brave Aegisthus, gone!

ORESTES:
You love this man? Then share his grave
and never betray him, even in death.

CLYTEMNESTRA:
Wait, my child! My son, have you no feelings?
This breast once nurtured you, cradled your sleep,
your soft mouth sucked the milk that made you strong.

ORESTES:
Pylades, what should I do? How can I kill my own mother?

(Enter Pylades from the doors)

PYLADES:
And what then becomes of the Oracles of Apollo
declared at Delphi, or the unbreakable oaths we took?
Better to be hated by every man on earth than hated by the gods.

ORESTES:
Your wise words have won me over, Pylades.

(To Clytemnestra)

Then come! I will slaughter you at his side.
Alive, you thought him better than my father.
Die then! And lie with him forever, your lover!
Since you hated the man you should have loved.

CLYTEMNESTRA:
I was the one who raised you; let me grow old with you.

ORESTES:
You killed my father, and now you want me to live with you?

CLYTEMNESTRA:
Destiny played a part in this, my son.

ORESTES:
Then Destiny shall make your deathbed.

893: "Aegisthus, gone!"—The body of Aegisthus was probably not present on stage at this point.

CLYTEMNESTRA:
You should fear the curse of your kin, my son.

ORESTES:
You just gave birth, then abandoned me to a life of misery.

CLYTEMNESTRA:
I never abandoned you. I sent you to the house of an ally.

ORESTES:
Sold like a slave, the son of a free man.

CLYTEMNESTRA:
Then where is the fee I received from the sale?

ORESTES:
I am ashamed to speak of it.

CLYTEMNESTRA:
Then you should also speak of your father's vices.

ORESTES:
Do not accuse him! He endured while you sat at home.

CLYTEMNESTRA:
My son, it is hard for a woman to be kept from her husband.

ORESTES:
It is a man's labor that provides the home you sit in.

CLYTEMNESTRA:
My son, I think you mean to kill your mother.

ORESTES:
You are the killer, not I. You kill yourself.

CLYTEMNESTRA:
Then beware the vengeful hellhounds of a mother's curse.

ORESTES:
And how would I escape a father's if I failed?

CLYTEMNESTRA:
I'm crying in vain over my own tomb.

ORESTES:
The fate of my father marked out your end.

CLYTEMNESTRA:
Ah! I suckled this serpent, I gave it life!

ORESTES:
Yes, the terror you saw in your dream was true.
You should not have killed, now suffer what you should not.

(Exit Clytemnestra, Orestes, and Pylades through the doors)

CHORUS:
Mourn for this pair and their double downfall,
but let all-enduring Orestes prevail
as he ascends this mountain of bloodshed.
Let the heart of this household never, ever die.

[Strophe 1]

Came justice at long last to Priam and his sons,
devastating retribution, payment in blood.
Came the double lion, a double god of war,
to the House of Agamemnon.
An exile, guided by Apollo,
steered by godly counsel,
to force this to its end.

[Mesode 1]

Raise the hallowed call for our master's house!
It has escaped the evil, it has been cleansed
of the two defilers, who wore the wealth away.
The House is free from its own foul fate.

[Antistrophe 1]

Came Hermes, secret fighter
who destroys with stealth,
his fighting hand held
by the true daughter of Zeus.
We call her Justice, rightly named,
breathing destruction, hatred and rage.

934: "Heart"—The Greek has "eye," which was regarded as the most precious and essential part of the body.

937: "The double lion"—a metaphor for Orestes and Pylades.

[Strophe 2]

Apollo ordained it, loud and clear
from the gorge at Mt. Parnassus.
He attacks by stealth, the time will come,
by stealth the wrong will be undone.
Always somehow, the gods prevail
to preserve us from these evils.
Heaven has the right to our respect.

[Mesode 2]

Now I can see the light,
the mighty curb that yoked the House
has been lifted. Rise up great House,
you have lain in ruins time enough.

[Antistrophe 2]

Time brings everything to fulfillment
as it threads the gates of this House,
cleansing the stain on the hearth,
the purifying rites driving out Ruin.
We see the face of fortune turn to favor,
the future looks bright to behold,
and the intruders are banished from the House.

(Enter Orestes from the doors, standing over the bodies of Aegisthus and Clytemnestra covered by the death shroud of Agamemnon)

ORESTES:
Look at the double tyrants of our country,
the killers of my father, the rapists of his House.
How regal they must have been, seated on their thrones,
and so much in love, even now, judging by their end.
They made their vows and stood by their pledges,
together they swore to murder my father,
together they swore they would die. They kept this faith.

Enter Orestes: The *ekkyklēma* may have been used here. This would make for an effective dramatic parallel with the tableau of Agamemnon and Cassandra displayed after *Agamemnon* 1371.

(Orestes indicates the cloth that killed Agamemnon.)

Look at this, as you try to comprehend the evil,
look at this hideous contrivance that fettered my father,
the manacles for his hands, the shackles for his feet.
Lay it out! Gather round!
Spread out the cloth that covered the man.
Let the father see, not mine, but the one that sees all,
let Helios the sun gaze at my mother's foul work.
He will be my witness on the judgment day
and testify that I was right to kill my mother.
As for Aegisthus, there is no need to speak of him,
he died the adulterer's death as set down by law.
She plotted this abomination against the man,
she, who bore his children, carried them in her womb.
Once there was love, but now you see the hatred, the evil.
What was she? A deadly serpent, a venomous viper
that poisoned by touch, leaving her prey unbitten.
Such an evil, audacious mind.
And this, what words can I find to describe it?
A trap for a wild animal, a shroud of death from head to foot,
a robe from the bath to cover a coffin.
No, it is a trawling mesh,
a hunting net, a garment to fetter the feet.
This is a robber's tool of the trade,
one who cheats guests and steals for gain,
luring victims with insolent stealth,
killing to gratify a treacherous heart.
I would have the gods destroy me, childless,
before I shared my house with a woman like this.

CHORUS:
Ai! What horrifying work!
What an abominable way to die!
Oh! Oh!
This pain will grow bitter fruit, the survivor will suffer!

ORESTES:
She did this, did she not? Mark my witness,
this shroud dyed by Aegisthus' sword.
The ravages of time and oozing blood

conspired to ruin this steeped embroidery.
Now I can praise him, now I can mourn him properly,
I can speak before the weaving that killed my father.
I grieve for our family, the things that were done, the suffering.
But do not envy me, I have won a tainted victory.

CHORUS:
No mortal man lives a life free from suffering.
No one exists only with honor.
Oh! Oh!
Day after day our lives are plagued by pain.

ORESTES:
I do not know how it will end.
I am a charioteer with a runaway team,
hurtling off the course, losing grip of the reins,
losing grip of my mind, spinning out of control.
My heart dances in terror and howls a furious tune.
While I still have my sanity, know this:
I killed my mother with Justice at my side.
She was a defiled murderer, the gods hated her.
What compelled me to do this? What magic charms?
The greatest influence was Apollo's prophet,
the oracle told me: "Do it and go unpunished,"
and if I had failed, the penalty defies description;
no arrow could reach the heights of those pains.
And now look at me, I have the suppliant's armor,
the olive branch and this wreath. I'll go to the sanctuary
at the center of the earth, the shrine of Loxian Apollo,
where the brilliant light of the sacred flame never dims.
I must run from the blood that I shed, run from my own blood,
no hearth will shelter me, only Delphi, it is Apollo's will.
I charge the men of Argos with remembrance:
tell Menelaus the evil things that happened here.
And now I go, an exile, banished from this land.
In life as in death, my name will always be known for this.

CHORUS:
But you have done well. Don't damn yourself
with evil words, don't let your tongue denounce you.

You have liberated the entire city of Argos
by beheading two snakes with one good clean stroke.

(Orestes imagines that he sees the Furies approaching.)

ORESTES:
Ah! Ah!
Women, there! Like Gorgons!
Black clad, writhing with snakes!
I can't stay here! I have to go!

CHORUS:
What is it? What sights whirl you into such a frenzy?
You are the son of Agamemnon, be still, don't surrender to fear.

ORESTES:
Not sights! These terrors are real!
The mother's curse, the hellhounds of hate, they are here!

CHORUS:
It must be the fresh blood on your hands,
you are distraught, confused.

ORESTES:
Lord Apollo! They are coming! Closing in!
I can see their eyes dripping with blood!

CHORUS:
You must be purified. The touch of Apollo
will free you from this torture.

ORESTES:
You can't see them, but I can, they force me away!
I must go now! Now!

(Exit Orestes, running through the stage left wing)

CHORUS:
Go with our blessings, Orestes. May the god protect you
and treat you kindly. May you be granted some good fortune.

Three times the storm has struck
and hurled its icy blasts

Orestes imagines: The Furies are probably not present on stage at this moment.

against this royal House.
First the feast of children's flesh,
Thyestes' tortured pain.
Then the murder of the man,
the deadly bath, the death of a king
who ruled the whole Greek army.
And now the third, it comes again,
the savior or the doom?
When will it end? When will it be calm?
When will it sleep, this fury, this Ruin?

(Exit the chorus through the stage right wing)

–END–

Exit the chorus: A tableau of the bodies of Clytemnestra and Aegisthus may have remained on stage as the final bloody image of the play, and then withdrawn behind the closing doors of the house to mark the end of the play, reflecting the close of *Agamemnon.*

EURIPIDES

Electra

Translated with Notes by Cecelia Eaton Luschnig

Cast of Characters

FARMER (unnamed)	Electra's husband
ELECTRA	
ORESTES	
CHORUS	of young Mycenaean women
OLD MAN	former personal slave of Agamemnon
MESSENGER	slave of Orestes
CLYTEMNESTRA	
DIOSCURI	Castor [and Polydeuces, nonspeaking] ex machina

Nonspeaking Roles

PYLADES	Orestes' companion
ENTOURAGE OF ORESTES	two or more slaves
SLAVES OF CLYTEMNESTRA	two or more Trojan women and two or more male attendants
POLYDEUCES	brother of Castor

Euripides' *Electra*

SCENE: *The Mycenaean countryside in front of the poor farmhouse of Electra's husband. The time is just before dawn. It is about seven years after the end of the Trojan War. The two* parodoi *(side entrances or wings) represent routes to the country (stage right) and the highway (stage left).*

Prologue

(Enter Farmer through the central doors.)

FARMER:
Earth's timeless soil, Inachus' streams,
here once King Agamemnon deployed the forces of war
and with a thousand ships sailed to the land of Troy.
On Trojan ground he killed old Priam, their king,
sacked the famous city Dardanus built,
and came home to Argos. On the high temples
he dedicated the lion's share of foreign spoils.
Over there he had success, but at home
he was killed by the treachery of his wife Clytemnestra

1: Inachus—the main river of the land of Argos. Like most rivers, he is a god.

5: Dardanus—the son of Zeus and Atlas' daughter Electra. He built the citadel of Troy and ruled over the Troad (Troy and the area around it). He was the ancestor of the kings of Troy down to Priam. Line 5 sets together the first and last of the kings of Troy. This is a favorite device in Greek poetry: at the end of a story, the poet takes us back to the beginning.

6: Argos and Mycenae are used interchangeably.

6–7: Spoils, in particular, refers to the armor stripped from dead enemies (see also 1000). Returning warriors nailed the armor to the temples. See Homer, *Iliad* 7.81–84, Herodotus, *The Histories* 5.95.1, Aeschylus, *Agamemnon* 577–79.

9: Clytemnestra—The original spelling was "Clytemestra" (without the "n"). The name means "renowned schemer" rather than "famously courted," which applies more aptly to her sister Helen .

and the hand of Thyestes' son Aegisthus.
He left behind the age-old scepter of Tantalus
when he died. Aegisthus is now king of the country
and keeps for himself Tyndareos' daughter, the late king's wife.
But *he* left his children at home when he sailed to Troy,
his son Orestes and a young daughter Electra—
the father's aged minder absconded with the boy
after Aegisthus resolved to kill him,
and gave him to Strophius to raise in the land of the Phocians.
But the girl Electra stayed behind in her father's halls,
until she ripened into a young woman, and suitors,
prominent men from all over Greece, came to court her.
In terror that she would marry well and bear a child
to avenge Agamemnon, Aegisthus kept her
in the house and would not let her marry any of them.
When even that strategy failed to ease his fear

11: "Age-old scepter"—The long history of Agamemnon's scepter is told in Homer's *Iliad* 2.102–9: it was made by Hephaestus and given by him to Zeus, who passed it on to Hermes, who gave it to Pelops. From Pelops it passed to his sons, first Atreus and then Thyestes, and finally to Atreus' son Agamemnon (see House of Pelops Family Tree). Tantalus was Pelops' father, but the Homeric scepter was never in his hands and is projected backward here. Agamemnon's scepter figures in Clytemnestra's dream in Sophocles' *Electra* (420). The Farmer takes a long view, showing interest in the generations of the people he mentions.

12: According to Homer, Aegisthus ruled for seven years until Orestes came back and slew his father's murderer (*Odyssey* 3.305–8). Exactly how Clytemnestra died is unclear in the *Odyssey.*

18: Strophius was married to Agamemnon's sister Anaxibia. He was king of Phocis (in central Greece; see map), where the Delphic sanctuary was located. Pylades was Strophius' son and Orestes' cousin. The two grew up together and were inseparable. Pylades is a presence in all three of the *Electra* plays, but has a speaking part (of three lines) only in Aeschylus' *Libation Bearers* (900–902). He has speaking parts in Euripides' *Orestes* and *Iphigenia among the Taurians*.

22–24: Aegisthus acted as Electra's *kurios* (guardian): Women, as a rule, did not act on their own in contractual matters (though Clytemnestra and Helen made second marital choices for themselves). Aegisthus clearly does not have Electra's best interest—nor that of her side of the family—at heart, and the farmer who receives Electra as his wife does not view Aegisthus as having the authority to give her in marriage.

that she might have children by a secret liaison with some noble,
he planned to kill her, but her mother, bloodthirsty
as she was, saved her from Aegisthus' hands.
For her husband's death she made an excuse, but she was afraid
the murder of her own child would cause an outcry.
Aegisthus had a brainstorm then—he put a price on the head
of Agamemnon's son, already in exile,
and *to me* he gave Electra to be my lawful
wedded wife. My people are Mycenaean;
there's no fault to be found on that score—
we are respectable but poor—
so much for good breeding! By giving her
to a poor man, he hoped to quell his fears.
If a man of rank had married her,
he would rouse the sleeping murder of Agamemnon
and at last Aegisthus would have gotten his just deserts.
I have never touched her—Aphrodite be my witness—
I could not shame her. Yes, Electra is still a virgin.
I was ashamed to lay rough hands on the daughter
of a wealthy family, being a working man myself.
I feel for poor Orestes, in name my kinsman,
if he ever comes home to Argos and sees
the miserable marriage they made for his sister.
And if anyone says I'm a fool to take a young
virgin into my home and not touch her,
he should know that he is measuring
right and wrong by false standards. He's the fool.

(Enter Electra through the central doors, carrying a hydria *[water vessel].)*

ELECTRA:
Black night, nurse of golden stars,
I go now to the running stream

33: "He gave Electra"—Up to this point the audience would be wondering who the Farmer is. He is not a mythological figure, not part of the traditional story, but an outsider, a person from contemporary society. This is an absolutely extraordinary fact.

Enter Electra: The characters are introduced in successive scenes of the prologue. Fetching water from the stream or springhouse is a traditional task for women.

with this jug balanced on my head,
not that I need to do such menial tasks,
but I want to show before the gods Aegisthus' insult
and let my laments for Father fly to heaven.
Tyndareos' daughter, my mother, damn her to hell,
threw me out of my home to please her husband.
Now she bears Aegisthus a new brood
and makes Orestes and me unwanted stepchildren.

FARMER:

Poor thing, why are you slaving away for my sake
and taking on chores, unsuited to the life you used to live,
and why don't you stop, even when I ask you to?

ELECTRA:

You are my true friend. I put you on a par with the gods
for not adding abuse to my troubles.
It's a great stroke of good fortune to find
relief from bad luck as I have found in you.
I must then, with whatever strength I can muster, without your asking,
try to lighten your load, so you can handle it more easily,
and to share your toils with you. You have enough work
outside. The household chores should be mine
to take care of. When a working man comes home
it is nice to find things inside in good order.

(Exit Electra, as she concludes this speech, stage right to the country.)

FARMER:

Go on, then, if you want to. It's not so far
from the house to the spring. But with the break of day
I must drive my oxen to my lands and sow my fields.
A lazy lout with the gods on his lips
cannot eke out a living except by working hard.

(Exit Farmer stage right to the country.)

75–76: This is the traditional division of labor in Greek society: women work mainly inside the house, men outside.

78: This line (see also 102) gives the time of day (daybreak) for the play's opening.

(Enter Orestes stage left from the highway with Pylades; two servants carry their baggage. Orestes is dressed in a fine traveler's cloak and a broad-brimmed hat.)

ORESTES:
Pylades, in my eyes you are first and foremost
my dearest, most loyal friend and host.
You alone of friends continue to respect Orestes
in my current situation, horrors brought on by Aegisthus
who killed my father with the help of that damnable woman,
my mother. I have come from the god's sacred rites
here to Argive land, in secret
to repay my father's murderers with death.
During the night just past I went to Father's grave,
shed tears, made an offering of my hair,
and slaughtered a sheep on the altar
in secret from the masters of this country.
I will not set foot inside the city-walls,
but have come to the country's borders
with two possibilities in mind: to leave
for another place if their spies get wind of me
and to look for my sister. I hear that she has been joined
in marriage and is no longer a virgin.
My plan is to find her and make her my accomplice in revenge
and thus gain knowledge about affairs inside the city.
Now that dawn is raising its white face,
let's get out of the road
in case some farmer or serving woman
shows up, so we can find out
if my sister lives anywhere nearby.
Look, I see a slave woman coming this way

(Electra comes into view and is heard singing.)

87: "The god's sacred rites"—The oracle at Delphi is central to Orestes' revenge plot, but in this play Apollo seems less involved. In Aeschylus' *Libation Bearers* (269–96), Apollo is most graphic in his pronouncements of what will happen to Orestes if he fails to avenge his father: physical torments, social ostracism, and visitation by the Furies. In Sophocles' *Electra*, Apollo's part is full but not clear. Orestes is told by the oracle to use deceit. Euripides' Orestes is vague about the content of the oracle.

carrying a heavy water jug on her shaved
head. Let's crouch down and listen
to this servant in case we can learn anything
about what we have come here for, Pylades.

(They hide behind the altar in the center of the orchestra.)

Electra's Monody

(Enter Electra stage right from the country, alone with the water jug on her head, singing.)

ELECTRA:

Hurry along—the time has come—
go on, go on in tears.
Ah, ah me.
I am Agamemnon's child,
and Tyndareos' loathsome daughter, Clytemnestra,
gave birth to me.
Down in the city, people
call me unhappy Electra.
Ah, ah for my never-ending toils
and hated life.
Father, you lie dead and gone,
slaughtered by your wife
and Aegisthus, O Agamemnon, my father.

Move on, waken the same refrain of sorrow,
raise high the pleasure that comes with mourning.

Hurry along—the time has come—
go on, go on in tears,
Ah, ah me.
In what city, in what house,
my poor brother, do you wander
leaving your sister
to the bitterest sorrows
in Father's chambers, mourning?
Come, release me from my life of misery,

108–9: "shaved head"—See note on 147–50.

131: "Do you wander"—"Are you a slave?" is another reading for this question.

from these toils.
Zeus, Zeus, bring ashore to Argos
the wanderer, the avenger
of Father's hideous bloodshed.

Take this vessel from my head and put it
on the ground. O Father, I cry out
in nightly keening.
A shrill wail, a song of death,
Father, I call to you, a song of death
down deep in the earth
with cries of grief I pass my days
forever, tearing at my neck,
dragging down my nails,
and beating my hands on
my head close-cropped for your death.

Aiai. Tear the head,
like a droning swan
beside running streams
that calls its own dear father
killed by the cunning snares
of nets, so I cry for you,
poor Father.

The last bath, your deathbed
bathed in blood—

140: "Take this vessel"—Does Electra have a slave, as some scholars believe, to whom she addresses these second-person imperatives, or does she speak to herself? In either case, she needs to have her hands free for the gestures of mourning.

147–50: Electra catalogs the rituals of mourning: her hair is shorn, she strikes her head, and she tears her skin with her nails.

151: "Like a droning swan"—Birds, especially swans, were admired by the Greeks for their filial piety. The swan was thought to sing in mourning and even in sorrow for its own impending death. Electra thinks of her father as snared by his wife, caught in deadly cloths (see Aeschylus, *Agamemnon* 1382–83).

157: "The last bath, your deathbed"—In Homer (*Odyssey* 4.534–35; 11.410–11) and Sophocles (*Electra* 203–7, 269), Agamemnon is killed at a banquet. Euripides' *Electra* (1148–49) follows Aeschylus' *Agamemnon* (1107–35).

ah me, ah me,
the bitter axe blow,
the bitter plot
you came home from Troy
your wife welcomed you
not with wreaths, not with crowns
but with merciless outrage she handed you over
to Aegisthus, his two-edged sword
and took the traitor as her lover.

(Enter the chorus along the parodoi, *from both directions.)*

Parodos

CHORUS:
Daughter of Agamemnon, Electra, I have come
to your rustic farmyard.
A stranger is here; a milk-drinking
mountain-roaming man has come from Mycenae.
He brings news that two days from now

160, 165: The axe is associated with Clytemnestra (in Aeschylus' *Libation Bearers* she calls for one when she realizes Orestes has returned, 889). In Homer, Agamemnon dies by the sword of Aegisthus (*Odyssey* 11.424). What weapon Clytemnestra used is not so clear in *Agamemnon*. In art, Aegisthus is usually depicted wielding a sword; Clytemnestra sometimes is shown with a sword and sometimes with an axe (Prag, Pl. 11c). In Sophocles, the instrument used by both Clytemnestra and Aegisthus is an axe (*Electra* 98–100, 193–96, 485). In Euripides, Clytemnestra uses an axe (160, 279, 1160), but Aegisthus wields a sword (165). It is possible that Clytemnestra killed him with an axe and Aegisthus mutilated him with the sword. The use of the axe, an instrument for killing an animal or felling a tree, dehumanizes the victim more than the sword, a weapon of war. On the mutilation, see Aeschylus, *Libation Bearers* (439); Sophocles, *Electra* (445–46); Euripides, *Electra* (164, *lōban,* "outrage").

167–212: Parodos—the entrance-song of the chorus.

169: "A stranger is here"—The man who brings the news of the festival is a herdsman, drinker of milk rather than wine. His life is so remote and he so poor that he lives off what his flock produces. Wine is the drink of the civilized. In Homer's *Odyssey,* the Cyclops is so uncivilized that Odysseus is able to overcome him with wine. (See Euripides, *Bacchae* 272–85 on the gifts of grain and grape.)

the Argives will proclaim a public sacrifice
and all the girls will march
in a procession of honor for Hera.

ELECTRA:

No, not for parties, my dear friends,
and not for golden rings
does my poor heart
take wing and I will not lead dances
with the Argive brides
or beat my whirling feet.
I spend the night in tears,
and mourning becomes me
in my daytime misery.
Look at my matted hair
and my dress in rags.
Are they fit for Agamemnon's
royal daughter
and for Troy, the city that can never forget
it was laid waste by my father?

CHORUS:

Hera is a great god. Come, now,
and borrow from me a fancy
dress to put on
and golden ornaments to grace its beauty.
Do you think if you do not honor the gods
you will defeat your enemies with your tears?
No, it's not with laments
but with prayers revering the gods
that you will reach your happy day, dear girl.

ELECTRA:

None of the gods hears the voice
of the unlucky, none cares about the ancient
butchery done to my father.
I cry for the one dead and gone
and for the living, the vagabond,

174: The *Heraia* (festival to Hera), which celebrates Hera's marriage to Zeus, was a major festival in Argos. The procession the chorus mentions is for unmarried girls.

who lives somewhere in another land,
unhappy wanderer
at the drudges' hearth,
son of a proud father.
And here in a poor man's hovel
I live, wasting away my life
banished from my father's house,
along these mountain crags,
while my mother lives in criminal marriage
with another husband.

First Episode

CHORUS:
So many troubles for all Greeks and for your own house
were brought on by your mother's sister Helen.

(Orestes and Pylades and their attendants get up from behind the altar.)

ELECTRA:
Oh my god! Women, I must break off these laments.
Some strangers are here near the house, lurking
behind the altar, and now they are getting up from their ambush;
run—you go back along the road and I'll head for the house—
we must try to escape from these outlaws.

ORESTES:
Wait, poor woman. Don't be afraid of me.

ELECTRA:
Phoebus Apollo, I beg you for my life.

ORESTES:
There are others I might kill, more my enemies than you.

ELECTRA:
Go away. Do not touch what you should not.

ORESTES:
There is no one I have more right to touch.

214: The reference to Helen may seem irrelevant, but the end of the play will reveal that assumptions about her guilt have been made for a purpose.

ELECTRA:
Why are you hiding there with a sword in your hand?

ORESTES:
Stay and listen. You'll be glad you did.

ELECTRA:
I'll stay. I'm in your power. You're stronger than me.

ORESTES:
I have come here with news from your brother.

ELECTRA:
My dear friend. Is he alive or dead?

ORESTES:
Alive. I'm happy to give the good news first.

ELECTRA:
Bless you. Thank you for this most welcome message.

ORESTES:
It is something we both share.

ELECTRA:
Where in the world is he living his dreary life of exile?

ORESTES:
He doesn't keep to one place but moves from city to city.

ELECTRA:
Does he have enough for his daily needs?

ORESTES:
That much he has, but a homeless man carries no weight.

ELECTRA:
What word of him do you bring?

ORESTES:
He wants to know if you are alive and if so in what condition.

ELECTRA:
First of all, do you see how drawn my skin is?

ORESTES:
Worn by your cares—it makes me want to cry.

ELECTRA:
And my head with the hair shaved off.

ORESTES:
You must miss your brother and your dead father.

ELECTRA:
Ah me, there is no one dearer to me than they.

ORESTES:
Ah! And your brother: don't you think he feels the same?

ELECTRA:
But he is away and not here with us.

ORESTES:
Why do you live out here so far from town?

ELECTRA:
I am married, stranger, a lethal match.

ORESTES:
I am sorry for your brother. Who is your husband?

ELECTRA:
Not a man my father expected to choose for me.

ORESTES:
Tell me so I can report it to your brother.

ELECTRA:
This is where I live, here at the border, in his house.

ORESTES:
Some dirt farmer or cowhand would live here.

241: "With the hair shaved off"—In Greek, *eskythismenon,* "scalped with a razor" (like a victim of the Scythians; see Herodotus, *The Histories* 4.64.2–3).

244: "Ah!"—In Greek, *pheu* is a cry of dismay or surprise, amounting almost to a gasp. Orestes utters exometric *pheu* after 261, 281, 366, and 968.

247: The word for "stranger" (*xenos*) means "friend in a foreign country, guest, host," so that Electra's term of address to her brother could also be translated as "my friend," but the irony of her having to call her brother "stranger" is maintained in the translation. At 83 Orestes calls Pylades both "friend" (*philos,* "loved one, family member") and "host" or "stranger" (*xenos*).

ELECTRA:
My husband is poor but decent and respectful to me.

ORESTES:
What form does your husband's respect take?

ELECTRA:
He has never taken advantage of me.

ORESTES:
Is it some sort of religious abstention or doesn't he care for you?

ELECTRA:
He did not think it right to insult my parents.

ORESTES:
And why didn't he count his blessings in making such a match?

ELECTRA:
He didn't think the man who gave me to him had authority, stranger.

ORESTES:
I understand. So he would not suffer Orestes' retribution.

ELECTRA:
He is aware of that, but he is also a decent man.

ORESTES:
Well, then, he must be one of nature's gentlemen. He deserves a good turn.

ELECTRA:
Yes, of course, if my missing brother ever comes home.

ORESTES:
Your own mother: did she put up with this?

ELECTRA:
Women's affections belong to their husbands, not their children, stranger.

ORESTES:
Why has Aegisthus insulted you in this way?

262: "Well, then"—This is another of Orestes' *pheus*; see note on 244.

ELECTRA:
By marrying me to such a man, he hoped I would have powerless children.

ORESTES:
So your children would not be able to take vengeance?

ELECTRA:
That was his ploy. I pray he will pay for it.

ORESTES:
Does you mother's husband know you are still a virgin?

ELECTRA:
No, he doesn't. We are keeping it a secret from him.

ORESTES:
And these women who are listening, are they friends?

ELECTRA:
Yes. They will keep their lips sealed.

ORESTES:
What, then, is Orestes' part in this if he comes to Argos?

ELECTRA:
You ask that! Shame on you. Isn't now the time for action?

ORESTES:
Then suppose he does come: how can he kill your father's murderers?

ELECTRA:
By doing to his enemies what they did to Father.

ORESTES:
Would you really have the heart to help him kill your mother?

ELECTRA:
With the same axe that killed my father.

ORESTES:
Should I tell him this, and that he can count on you?

ELECTRA:
Let me die once I have shed my mother's blood.

ORESTES:
Ah, if only Orestes were nearby to hear this.

ELECTRA:
But, you know, I wouldn't recognize him if I saw him.

ORESTES:
I'm not surprised. You were both very young when you were separated.

ELECTRA:
Only one person I know would recognize him.

ORESTES:
The one they say saved him from being murdered?

ELECTRA:
Yes: my father's old childhood slave.

ORESTES:
Did your father get a decent burial when he died?

ELECTRA:
He got what he got, flung out as he was from the house.

ORESTES:
What a story! Even strangers' troubles
can actually make a person feel pain.
Go on with your tale so I can tell your brother
the news, unwelcome, but he needs to hear it.
Pity is not found in boorish ignorance,
but in men of finer feelings; and even for the sensitive,
too much sensitivity has to have its price.

CHORUS:
I have the same longing in my heart too.
We live far from town and do not know
the troubles in the city, but want to learn them now.

ELECTRA:
I'll tell—or should I?—yes, you are a friend so I must tell
the heavy fortune that has struck me and my father.
Since you press me to tell the tale, stranger, I beg you,
bring news to Orestes of my troubles and his own.
First, look at the rags I am kept in, here in this stable,
how much grime I am weighed down with, under what roof
I live after my home in the royal palace.
I have to toil at weaving my own clothes

or else go naked and do without
and I carry water from the spring myself.
I live in privation, without sacred festivals and dances,
and shrink from the company of women because I'm still a virgin,
and I am ashamed to face Castor, my kinsman
to whom I was betrothed before he went up to the gods.
But my mother, decked out with the spoils of Phrygia,
sits on her throne, and beside her are stationed
slave women, my father's captives,
in Trojan gowns fastened with golden pins.
While in my home Father's blood is still
putrefied to black and his murderer
goes driving in the same chariot Father used,
and the scepter with which Father commanded the Greek armies,
he swaggers around holding it in his blood-drenched hands.
And Agamemnon's burial mound lies dishonored
and never received libations or boughs of myrtle
and his altar stands neglected, without offerings.
Meanwhile the rumor is that mother's splendid husband
gets drunk, leaps on his grave, and throws rocks at Father's headstone
and has the gall to utter these words to mock us:
"Where is your boy Orestes? Is he here to protect your tomb
like a good son?" This is how he is insulted because he's not here.

312–13: The betrothal of Electra to her uncle (a degree of consanguinity allowed by Athenian marriage practice) may be an invention of Euripides. Castor and Polydeuces (Pollux) were the twin sons of Zeus and Leda (*Dioscuri;* in Latin, *Gemini*), one mortal, one divine. When Castor died, they were allowed to share immortality as stars and protectors of sailors.

314–17: Phrygia and Phrygians are metonymies for Troy and Trojans, respectively.

324: Myrtle is an aromatic evergreen shrub (genus *Myrtus*), native to the Mediterranean region, and is a favorite plant for various kinds of ceremonial decoration.

326–31: Electra's description of Aegisthus at the tomb mocking her father is based on rumor as she admits (327 lit., "so they say") and contrasts strongly with the gracious Aegisthus we meet in the reported scene.

But, stranger, please, bring him this report.
Its senders are many and I speak for them,
my hands, my lips, my broken heart;
my shorn head and his own father.
It is a disgrace if Father wiped out the Trojans,
but *he,* one on one, cannot kill this man,
though he is young and born of a nobler father.

CHORUS:
I see him, your husband, I mean.
He has left his work and is heading home.

(Enter Farmer stage right from the country.)

FARMER:
What's this? Who are these strangers I see in front of my door?
Why have they come out here to my house in the country?
Are they looking for me? It's not proper, you know,
for a woman to be in the company of young men.

ELECTRA:
Oh no, dear, do not be suspicious of me.
Let me tell you what their story is. These strangers
have come from Orestes to bring me news of him.

(To Orestes and Pylades.)

Please, excuse what he just said.

FARMER:
What do they have to say? Is he alive?

ELECTRA:
Yes, at least that's what they say and I have no reason to distrust them.

FARMER:
And does he keep in mind what was done to his father and you?

341–400: The Farmer and Orestes do not engage with each other. The Farmer addresses Orestes, but Orestes does not answer him directly, showing a class distinction.

344: In Athenian society, women were secluded. It was the man's job to negotiate with strangers. The social norms are defied in tragic action, which takes place at the gates of the scene building and thus requires that the female characters be outside.

ELECTRA:
That's what I hope. But a man in exile is powerless.

FARMER:
What news have they brought of Orestes?

ELECTRA:
He sent them to observe my troubles.

FARMER:
Well, some they can see. The rest, I imagine, you told them.

ELECTRA:
Yes, they know. They have no deficiency on that score.

FARMER:
Why haven't we opened our doors to them by now?
Please, go into the house. For your welcome news
you will receive whatever hospitality my house can offer.

(To Orestes' attendants.)

Go on and take the baggage inside my house.

(To Orestes.)

And don't say no. You come as friends
from a friend. Even if I am a poor man,
I will not show a mean spirit.

ORESTES:
My god, is this the man who helps you mask
your marriage, to spare Orestes' good name?

ELECTRA:
He is called unhappy Electra's husband.

ORESTES:
Ah, there are no easy answers in the matter of a man's worth.
Human nature is beyond comprehension.
In the past I've seen the son of a noble father
amount to nothing and outstanding children born of worthless men.
I've seen the poverty of a rich man's mind
and a keen intellect in a poor man's body.
[How is anyone to make a correct distinction?
According to wealth? Then he'll be relying on a corrupt judge.

By lack, then? But poverty carries its own disease:
it leads a man to crime because of need.
But should I use military prowess? Can anyone face a spear
and bear witness to another's valor?
No, it's best to leave these things to fall as they may.]
This man is nobody of importance in Argos;
he can claim no distinction of family.
He may be common as dirt, but he's a man of quality.
Why not be sensible, instead of deceiving ourselves
with empty speculations, and judge people
by associating with them and knowing their character?
[This is the kind of man who could manage a city or home
well. But empty muscle men without a brain
are only good for statues in the public square. The strong arm
does not hold out against the spear any better than the weak
but it is a matter of a man's nature and his mettle.]
The son of Agamemnon who sent us
is worthy, whether he is here or not,
so let us enjoy the hospitality of this house.

(To his servants.)

You may go
into the house. I'll take a poor but considerate man
as my host over a rich one.

(Exit servants into the house with baggage.)

I accept the invitation into this man's house,
but I would prefer to have your brother
receive me into a prosperous home in happier circumstances.
Maybe he will come. The oracles of Loxias
are certain. Though for human fortune telling I have no use.

(Exit Orestes and Pylades through the central doors into the house.)

373–79: Square brackets [ ] around lines in the translation indicate sections of doubtful authenticity, especially those scholars suspect of being interpolations made for later productions as this one is (see Page 1934, pp. 74–75) or editors' notes that crept into the text from the margins.

399: Loxias—Apollo in his role as prophet.

CHORUS:
Now more than before, Electra, my heart is warming
with joy. Maybe now at last
your fortune is looking up and will turn out well.

ELECTRA: *(To her husband.)*
You fool, you know how poor we are. How could you invite
these guests who are so much better off than you?

FARMER:
What's this? If they are as well-bred as they seem,
won't they be just as content with the meager as the plentiful?

ELECTRA:
Meager is what you have! But since you have made this blunder,
go to my father's dear old childhood slave
who was cast out of the city and keeps sheep for company
near the Tanaus River where it forms the border
between Argive and Spartan territory.
Tell him that guests have come and he should bring
something for the strangers' dinner.

(Farmer starts to object.)

Oh, he'll be glad, I assure you, and he'll thank the gods
when he hears the infant he saved all those years ago is still alive.
We would get nothing out of our ancestral home
from Mother. It's bitter news we would bring her
if that awful woman learned that Orestes is alive.

FARMER:
Well, if you think so, I'll take the news
to the old man. But hurry on in
and get things ready inside.

(Exit Electra into the house.)

If she wants to, a woman
can find plenty to serve for a meal.
There is still enough in my house
to fill their bellies for a day.
When my mind falls to thinking this way
I consider what great power money has—
to give to strangers and when you fall ill

to pay for medicines. To sustain yourself
day to day doesn't cost a lot. Everybody,
rich or poor, can only hold so much.

(Exit Farmer stage left to the highway.)

First Stasimon

CHORUS:

[Strophe 1]

Famous ships that sailed once to Troy
with oars too many to count,
escorting the chorus of Nereid nymphs.
To the music of the pipe a dolphin leapt alongside them
whirling around the dark prows
bringing the son of Thetis,
swift Achilles, nimble of foot,
to accompany Agamemnon
to the banks of Simois in Troy.

[Antistrophe 1]

Nereids leaving Euboean headlands
carried the armorers' toils from the anvils
of Hephaestus—golden armor
up Pelion's slopes, up through the woodlands of Ossa
searching for high lookouts of nymphs
where the Centaur Chiron like a father
raised a bright light for Hellas,
the sea goddess Thetis' swift-footed
son, for the sons of Atreus.

434: Nereids are sea nymphs, daughters of Nereus, sisters of Achilles' mother, Thetis.

444: In Homer, the set of body armor made by Hephaestus (*Iliad* 18) is very different from that described here and is brought to Achilles in Troy by his mother after his first set was worn into battle by Patroclus and stripped from his fallen body.

445: Pelion—the site of the wedding of Achilles' parents, Peleus and Thetis, and the home of Chiron, the Centaur who reared and educated Achilles and other heroes.

[Strophe 2]

I heard from someone in the port, back from Troy
who had come to Nauplia,
how in the circle of your famous shield,
son of Thetis,
these icons were forged,
terrors for the Phrygians:
around the surface of the rim
Perseus above the sea on winged sandals
holds the Gorgon's severed head
in the company of Hermes, Zeus' messenger,
the rustic son of Maia.

[Antistrophe 2]

Shining in the middle of the shield there glinted
the sun's orb
mounted on heavenly horses
and the ethereal choreographies of stars:
Pleiades and Hyades, causing
Hector to turn away his eyes;
and on the helmet made of gold
Sphinxes bearing in their talons
their deadly song's prey
and on the breastplate's rounded form, breathing fire
the Chimera raced on her lion's claws
peering up at Pegasus, the flying colt of Peirene.

[Epode]

On the stabbing sword galloped
four-footed horses, black dust swirling over their backs.

460–63: A direct look at the Gorgon, Medusa, turned people into stone. Perseus used mirrors to see her face, slew her, and carried her head around. Later he gave the head to Athena.

471–75: A Sphinx is a bird-woman who brings death. The Theban Sphinx sang a riddle and seized and devoured men who could not solve it, until Oedipus guessed it right.

474: Chimera is a compound female monster made up of lioness, goat, and snake who breathes fire. She was killed by Bellerophon with the help of Pegasus, the colt of Peirene, the winged horse that sprang from the Gorgon (Medusa) when Perseus beheaded her.

The king of those great men in arms
your marriage killed,
evil-minded daughter of Tyndareos.
For that, one day, the gods in heaven
will dispatch you to death. Truly one day
to come I will see the blood of murder
pouring out beneath your neck
gashed by the sword.

Second Episode

(Enter Old Man, pulling a sheep and carrying provisions, stage left from the highway.)

OLD MAN:
Where is she? Where is my young lady, my mistress,
daughter of Agamemnon, him that I brought up myself?
What a steep climb she has up to her house
for a shriveled old man like me to get to on foot.
Still, she is dear to me and on my wobbly knees
I must drag along this hunched back.
Hello, daughter, now I see you there in front of the house.
I'm here to bring you a young lamb
from my flock—here it is, the one I picked
and wreaths and some cheese from the press
and this precious vintage wine full of aroma,
just a drop, but something sweet to add,
a cup or so, to a weaker drink.
Someone go and bring this to the guests inside.
I have to lift my ragged cloak and wipe
my eyes that are drenched with tears.

ELECTRA:
Why are your eyes dripping with tears, old man?
Does my situation remind you of your troubles after all this time?
Or do you weep over Orestes' hard exile
and my father you once held in your arms
and cared for, in vain for yourself and those you love?

OLD MAN:
In vain, that's right. Still I did not hold back.
I took a detour to visit his tomb,

and I knelt down and wept at seeing it deserted;
then I opened the wineskin I'm carrying for your guests
and poured a libation and I covered his mound with myrtle.
There on the altar I saw a sacrificed sheep,
a black one for the dead, and blood spilled not long ago.
There were locks of hair cut in mourning.
I was amazed, my girl, to think who in the world dared
to visit the tomb. No Argive would have, that's for sure.
Look here, maybe your brother has come in secret
and paid respect to his father's neglected grave.
Go look at the hair. Put it next to your own
to see if the color is the same as yours.
It often happens that people with the same father
have many physical traits in common.

ELECTRA:
What you are saying makes you sound stupid, old man,
if you think my brave brother has come
to the country in secret out of fear of Aegisthus.
Will two locks of hair be alike,
one from the head of a noble youth raised in the wrestling schools,
the other a woman's and well-combed? It's absurd.
Besides, many people have hair the same color
who do not share the same blood, old man.

OLD MAN:
Well then, why don't you go to where I saw his footprint
and see if it's the same size as your own, child?

ELECTRA:
How could his feet leave an impression
in the rocky ground? And even if there is,
the feet of brother and sister, a man and a woman,
would not be alike. The man's are bigger.

OLD MAN:
If your brother has entered the country, is there any way
you could recognize him by some weaving from your loom
in which once long ago I stole him away from imminent death?

515–46: The cut lock of hair, the footprint, and the weaving are the tokens of recognition in Aeschylus' *Libation Bearers* (167–234).

ELECTRA:

Don't you know that I was a child when Orestes
went into exile? And even if I was already weaving cloth,
he was only a baby then. How could he still be wearing
the same clothes, unless they grew to keep up with him?
But either some stranger took pity on the grave
and cut his hair or they were sent to spy out the land.

OLD MAN:

Where are the strangers? I want to see them
and ask them about your brother.

ELECTRA:

Here they are, coming out of the house with quick steps.

OLD MAN:

They look well-born, but there's no telling from looks.
Many well-born men are worthless.
Still, I bid the visitors good day.

ORESTES:

Greetings, old man. Really, Electra, this antique relic
of a man, who in the world is he?

ELECTRA:

This, stranger, is the man who tended my father.

ORESTES:

What? Is he the one who spirited away your brother?

ELECTRA:

Yes, he is the one who saved him, if he is still alive.

ORESTES:

Ah, why is he staring at me as if he is examining
the shiny imprint on a coin? Do I remind him of someone?

ELECTRA:

Maybe he is happy to see someone Orestes' age.

ORESTES:

Well, Orestes is a friend of mine. Why is he walking around me?

546: Textual problems make it uncertain what Euripides wrote here or what exactly "they" refers to.

ELECTRA:
I'm wondering about that, too, stranger.

OLD MAN:
My lady, dear daughter, Electra, praise the gods.

ELECTRA:
Why? What for, of all that is possible in the world?

OLD MAN:
For the thing you most desire, which god is revealing.

ELECTRA: *(Electra gestures, raises arms in prayer.)*
There, I call on the gods. Or what do you mean, old man?

OLD MAN:
Look at this man, my child, the man closest to you.

ELECTRA:
I have been looking at him for quite a while. Are you all right?

OLD MAN:
Of course I'm all right. I am looking at your brother.

ELECTRA:
What do you mean, old man, by this astonishing statement?

OLD MAN:
That I see Orestes right here: Agamemnon's son.

ELECTRA:
What sign do you see that I can trust?

OLD MAN:
See the scar over his eyebrow? He got that in your father's house
one day when he fell and bloodied it, while you two were chasing a deer.

ELECTRA:
What are you saying? Yes, I do see a scar from an accident.

OLD MAN:
Do you hesitate to embrace your dearest brother?

573–74: In Homer's *Odyssey* (19.390–475), Odysseus' old nurse recognizes him because of a scar. Odysseus in turn uses it to identify himself to his herdsmen (21.217–19).

ELECTRA:
Not any more, old man. I am convinced in my heart
by your token of recognition. *(Embracing Orestes.)* I hold you
at last, against all hope.

ORESTES:
And at last you are in my arms.

ELECTRA:
Never expected.

ORESTES:
I dared not hope.

ELECTRA:
Are you he?

ORESTES:
Yes, your only ally
If I pull in the catch I am going after . . . and I am confident.
Or else we should stop believing in the gods,
if wrong triumphs over right in the end.

Choral Interlude

CHORUS:
You have come, you have come, long-awaited day,
you have shone down, you have revealed to the city
a beacon in blazing light, who in long exile
from his father's house
was wandering in misery.
Now some god, yes, a god brings us
victory, my dear.
Raise up your hands, raise your voice in prayers
lifted to the gods that your brother
will enter the city in good fortune.

Second Episode: Continued

ORESTES:
Well. I have enjoyed the sweet pleasure
of your embraces and in time we will share them again.
But, you, old man, you have arrived in good time.
Tell me, what should I do to take revenge on Father's murderer

and my mother, his partner in unholy marriage?
Are there any in Argos kindly disposed toward me,
or, like my luck, am I completely bankrupt?
Who are my allies? Should I act at night or in the daylight?
What road can we take against our enemies?

OLD MAN:
Son, you have no friends when your luck runs out.
It is a rare find, you know, if you have someone
to share in common both good times and bad.
In the eyes of your friends you are totally ruined
and have left them no hope. But listen to me:
you hold in your own hands and in fortune everything
you need to recover your estate and your city.

ORESTES:
What must I do to reach this goal?

OLD MAN:
Kill Thyestes' son and your mother.

ORESTES:
This is the crown I have come here for, but how do I get it?

OLD MAN:
Even if you wanted to, *not* by going inside the city walls.

ORESTES:
Is he surrounded by a garrison and bodyguards?

OLD MAN:
That's right. He lives in fear and does not sleep soundly.

ORESTES:
Good. Old man, you plan the next step.

OLD MAN:
Wait. Listen. I just remembered something.

ORESTES:
Tell me some good news. I would be happy to hear it.

OLD MAN:
I saw Aegisthus on my way here.

ORESTES:
I'm very glad to hear this. Where was he?

OLD MAN:
Where he pastures his horses, not far from this farm.

ORESTES:
What was he doing? I see hope coming out of my helplessness.

OLD MAN:
I think he was preparing a festival to the Nymphs.

ORESTES:
For bringing up a child or a coming birth?

OLD MAN:
I don't know, but he came prepared to slaughter a bull.

ORESTES:
How big was their party or did he just have his household slaves?

OLD MAN:
No Argive citizens were there, just a bunch of his slaves.

ORESTES:
I don't suppose there's anybody who will recognize me, old man.

OLD MAN:
They are slaves who've never seen you.

ORESTES:
Would they be disposed toward us if we succeed?

OLD MAN:
That's the character of slaves, and a bonus for you.

ORESTES:
So how can I get close to him?

OLD MAN:
Go where he'll see you as he is sacrificing.

ORESTES:
It looks like he has his lands right off the road?

625: Mountain Nymphs are divinities of springs and are worshiped at specific locations. They are associated with fertility, childbirth, and good health ("nymph" means "bride"). Line 626 hints that Clytemnestra might be pregnant.

OLD MAN:
Yes, and when he sees you there, he'll invite you to join the feast.

ORESTES:
A distasteful dinner guest, god willing.

OLD MAN:
From there you must look to the throw of the dice.

ORESTES:
Good. Thank you. But my mother—where is she?

OLD MAN:
In Argos; but she will join her husband for the sacrifice.

ORESTES:
Why didn't she set out with Aegisthus?

OLD MAN:
She stayed behind out of fear of public censure.

ORESTES:
Of course. She must know she is an object of suspicion in town.

OLD MAN:
That's so. Everybody detests an immoral woman.

ORESTES:
How will I kill her and him with one blow?

ELECTRA:
I will take care of the murder of my mother.

ORESTES:
With him so close, luck is surely on my side.

ELECTRA: *(Pointing to Old Man.)*
Let him be assistant to both of us.

OLD MAN:
I'll do that. What manner of death do you have in mind for your mother?

ELECTRA:
Old man, go tell this story to Clytemnestra:
bring her news that I have just given birth to a baby boy.

OLD MAN:
Was the birth a while ago or just now?

ELECTRA:
Ten days ago, the time it takes for a new mother to be purified.

OLD MAN:
And how exactly does this bring about your mother's death?

ELECTRA:
She will come when she hears I am indisposed from the birth.

OLD MAN:
Why do you think she cares about you, dear child?

ELECTRA:
She does. And she will shed real tears over the baby's status.

OLD MAN:
Maybe so, but bring your story back to the goal.

ELECTRA:
When she gets here, obviously, she dies.

OLD MAN:
She will come right to the doors of your house.

ELECTRA:
And from there it is just a small step to Hell.

OLD MAN:
Once I have seen this I'll die a happy man.

ELECTRA:
First, old man, show him the way.

OLD MAN:
Where Aegisthus is sacrificing to the gods?

ELECTRA:
Yes—then go find my mother and tell her my news.

OLD MAN:
She will think she is hearing it from your own lips.

ELECTRA: *(To Orestes.)*
It's your work now. You have drawn the first killing.

654: A woman was considered ritually unclean through the labor, during the birth, and for ten days after the birth. On the tenth day, the baby was named and acknowledged as a member of the family.

ORESTES:
I'm off, if he will guide me there.

OLD MAN:
Yes, I am happy to show you the way.

ORESTES:
Zeus of my ancestors, defend me against my enemies.

ELECTRA:
Pity us; our suffering makes us worthy of your pity.

OLD MAN:
Pity your descendants.

ELECTRA:
And Hera, you have power over Mycenae's altars.

ORESTES:
Grant us victory, if what we ask is right.

OLD MAN:
Grant justice in requital for their father's death.

ORESTES:
And you, Father, foully murdered living down below in the earth . . .

ELECTRA:
And Earth, queen of all, I strike with my hands.

OLD MAN:
Defend these dear, dear children, defend them.

ORESTES:
Come now, bring armies of the dead as our allies.

ELECTRA:
Those who with you annihilated the Phrygians in war.

OLD MAN:
All who abhor the unholy polluters.

ORESTES:
Do you hear, Father, you who suffered outrage from Mother?

OLD MAN:
Your father hears all this. Time now to go.

ELECTRA:

And so I declare to you: Aegisthus must die.
Since if you go down, pinned in a fatal fall,
I'm dead, too; don't speak of me as being alive,
for I shall stab myself in the heart with a two-edged sword.
I am going inside to get ready
so that if good news of you comes the whole house
will lift its voice in songs of thanksgiving, but if it is news
of your death, the opposite. This is what I had to say to you.

ORESTES:

I know all I need to know.

ELECTRA:

For this, you must be a man.

(Exit Orestes with Old Man, accompanied by Pylades and the servants, stage left.)

But you, women, kindle a torch to shout
the outcome of this contest, and I will stand watch,
holding a sword ready in my hand,
and never, if I am overwhelmed by my enemies,
I will *never* allow them the satisfaction of abusing me while I'm alive.

(Exit Electra through the central doors into the house.)

Second Stasimon

CHORUS:

[Strophe 1]

This myth is told in shadowy rumors
that once in the Argive
mountains Pan, steward of fields,

686: "Pinned in a fatal fall"—a metaphor from wrestling. See Aeschylus, *Agamemnon* 171–72.

688: For "heart" the manuscripts have "head," which has been emended to either "liver" or "heart." This is a masculine manner of suicide, but women sometimes threaten to use it; in ancient Greek literature, a woman's favored method of suicide was hanging (see Loraux 1987, pp. 14, 54).

689–93: Some scholars suspect that these lines, seen as bathetic rather than pathetic, are interpolations by actors or producers (Page 1934, pp. 75–76).

blowing sweet music
on well-pitched pipes,
brought a lamb with
gorgeous golden fleece from its tender mother.
And standing on the stone steps
the herald cried,
"To the square, to the square,
Mycenaeans, come all, to see
the marvel, the blessed kings'
portent." With dances they celebrated
the houses of the sons of Atreus.

[Antistrophe 1]

Fire-pans worked with gold were spread
up and down the town—fires gleamed
on the altars of the Argives.
The lotus reed, servant of the Muses,
piped in melodious voice.
Sweet songs swelled
celebrating the golden lamb. A new ending
for Thyestes' story: in a secret liaison
he had seduced the dear wife
of Atreus and brought the marvel
home. Walking then
among the assembled people he proclaims
that he has in his house
the horned sheep with golden wool.

[Strophe 2]

Then, it was then that Zeus changed
the shining orbits of the stars
and the fire of the sun

700–706: Pan—the god of fields and forests who pipes to his flocks on the panpipes, a rustic instrument of graduated reeds.

718–19: "A new ending / for Thyestes' story"—The meaning of the word *epilogoi* in the manuscripts is doubtful. Emendations include "then came Thyestes' trick"; "in praise of the golden lamb"; "Thyestes had the luck."

726–36: The sun used to set in the east, but Zeus changed its course in outrage at Thyestes' crime. See Plato, *Statesman (Politicus)* 268e–269a.

and the pale face of dawn,
and he harried the western expanses
with hot god-fanned flame;
in the north, rain-filled clouds,
but the arid ground of Ammon Ra
withers without moisture,
deprived of beautiful rains from Zeus.

[Antistrophe 2]

So it is told, but in my eyes
it carries little credence
that the golden-faced sun
reversed course and moved
the torrid zone
to afflict the mortal race
for the sake of human justice.
Frightening myths are a blessing
for mankind and advance the gods' service.
Forgetful of them, you killed
your husband, sister of celebrated brothers.

Third Episode

(Loud shouting is heard in the distance.)

CHORUS:
What's that!
Friends, did you hear a shout—or has some vain impulse
come over me? Like Zeus' rumbling from under the ground.
Listen, these rising winds must mean something.
Electra, come out of the house, dear lady.

ELECTRA:
Friends, what is it? How have we come out in the contest?

734: Ammon Ra—the oracle of Ammon (Amun) at the oasis of Siwa in the desert of Libya.

746: "Sister of celebrated brothers"—this probably refers to Clytemnestra as sister of the Dioscuri (Castor and Polydeuces).

748: "Zeus' rumbling"—Earthquakes are caused by Poseidon, but here the sound of an earthquake (subterranean or seismic rumblings) is compared to thunder, which comes from Zeus.

CHORUS:
All I know is that I just heard a scream of murder.

ELECTRA:
I heard it too, but from far away.

CHORUS:
The sound comes a long way, but still it is sharp.

ELECTRA:
Is the cry Argive or from those I love?

CHORUS:
I cannot tell. It's just noise. The words are all mixed up.

ELECTRA:
You announce my death. Why delay?

CHORUS:
Wait until you learn your fate more clearly.

ELECTRA:
No. We are defeated. Where are the messengers?

CHORUS:
They will be here. It's no trivial matter to kill a king.

(Enter Messenger stage left.)

MESSENGER:
Women of Mycenae, happy in victory,
I bring news of Orestes' triumph to all who love him:
Agamemnon's murderer, Aegisthus, lies dead
on the ground. Let us praise the gods.

ELECTRA:
Who are you? Why should I believe what you are telling me?

759: The choral ode covers an indeterminate passage of time during which Aegisthus is killed while the chorus sings of the crime of his father Thyestes that started the interfilial feud. Messengers often seem to arrive at the end of an ode, too soon after an event. This question may be a metatheatrical allusion to the stage convention or an indication of Electra's impatience or anxiety.

765: Of the twenty-six messengers in Greek tragedy, this is the only one whose truthfulness is questioned.

MESSENGER:
Don't you recognize your brother's servant when you see him?

ELECTRA:
Dear, dear man. I was so terrified that I could not recognize
your face. Now I know who you are. What are you saying?
Is he really and truly dead, the hated murderer of my father?

MESSENGER:
He is dead. A second time I tell you what you want to hear.

ELECTRA:
O gods and Justice that sees all, at last you have come!
Tell me the manner and order of events
in which he killed Thyestes' son. I want to hear it.

MESSENGER:
When we left this house
we walked along a rutted wagon trail
to where the "illustrious" king of the Mycenaeans was.
In fact he had gone into a well-watered garden
and was cutting sprays of young myrtle for his head.
When he saw us, he called out, "Hello, strangers, who are you?
Where are you traveling from? What country do you call home?"
And Orestes answered, "We are Thessalians. We are going
to the Alpheus River to sacrifice to Olympian Zeus."
When he heard that, Aegisthus continued,
"Now you must join us here at our hearth
and share the sacrifice with me. I am slaughtering a bullock
to the Nymphs. At dawn after a good night's sleep
you can start out from here refreshed. Come, let's go in."
And just as he was saying this, he took us by the hand
and led us off the road with the words, "You can*not* say no."
When we were inside, he went on, saying to his servants,
"Hurry, one of you, and bring water for the strangers' hands

791–837: This is a fairly complete documentation of the ritual of sacrifice: the ritual washing, the carrying in of the implements for sacrifice, the throwing of barley from the basket onto the altar, the cutting of hair from the victim, the raising of the animal (if it is small enough) and the cutting of its throat, the butchering, the inspection of the liver (at this point, the sacrifice is cut short) for omens, roasting, libations of wine, and the sharing of the meat (see Burkert 1985, pp. 56–59, 112–13).

so they can stand at the altar beside the lustral bowl."
But Orestes broke in, "We washed just now
in pure water from a flowing river.
If strangers are permitted to join in sacrifice with citizens,
King Aegisthus, we are ready and will not say no."
This conversation took place in the midst of the company.
Setting aside their spears, their master's defense,
all the servants set their hands to the task:
some brought bowls for the blood, others lifted the baskets,
others lit the fire, and around the sacrificial altars
some were setting up basins. The whole building was abuzz.
Then your mother's husband took the barley cakes
and threw them on the altars with these words,
"Nymphs of the rocks, I pray that with my wife,
the daughter of Tyndareos, I may continue to sacrifice,
in prosperity as I do now, but for my enemies nothing of the sort,"
meaning Orestes and you. My master, of course,
without speaking the words out loud, prayed the opposite,
to recover his father's house. Aegisthus took a straight-bladed knife
out of the basket and cut a tuft of the calf's hair
and placed it on the fire with his right hand,
and he cut its throat while servants hoisted the beast up
on their shoulders. Then he said to your brother,
"The Thessalians boast that it is a sign
of merit, if anyone excels at butchering a bull
or at breaking in horses. Here, stranger, take the sword
and show us that the legend about Thessaly's men is true."
Orestes took the well-made Dorian sword,
threw off his fine traveling cloak,
and, taking Pylades as his assistant in the work,
he made the servants stand aside. Grabbing hold of the calf's hoof,
he reached out, bared the white flesh,
and skinned off the hide quicker
than a racer on horseback completes a double track.
Then he loosened the flanks. Aegisthus took the sacred parts
in his hands and examined them. The lobe of the liver
was missing. The portal vein and gallbladder next to it
revealed to him ordeals of ill omen.
His face clouded over, and my master asked him,
"Is something troubling you?" "Stranger, I am in terror

of some treachery from outside. Agamemnon's son
is my worst enemy, and he is at war with my house."
To this Orestes said, "Do you really fear the treachery of an exile,
and you king of the city? Let's get ready for the feast—
will somebody bring us a Phthian cleaver
instead of this Dorian so I can break open the breastbone?"
He took it in his hands and struck. Aegisthus was still holding
the guts,
scrutinizing them, trying to sort them out. As he was nodding
over them, your brother, standing on tiptoe,
struck his vertebrae and smashed the joints
of his back. His whole body convulsed up and down
and he bellowed in the throes of a horrific death.
When they saw what was happening, the slaves rushed to arms,
a lot of them for two to fight against. With a show of courage
Pylades and Orestes took their stand, brandishing weapons
in the face of the mob. And he said, "I have not come
as an enemy to the city or my former comrades.
I have avenged myself on my father's killer.
I am the misused Orestes. Do not kill me.
You were my father's servants in days past." Hearing his words,
they stayed their spears. And he was recognized
by an old man from the household.
They started at once to crown your brother's head,
rejoicing and raising a happy cry. He is coming now,
bringing not the Gorgon's head to show you,
but Aegisthus whom you hate. Blood has now been shed
in bitter repayment for the blood of the dead man.

Choral Dance

CHORUS:

[Strophe]

Set your feet to dancing, dear,
like a fawn skipping up

836: "Phthian cleaver"—a butcher knife.

839: "As he was nodding"—At a sacrifice the victim is made to nod as if assenting to its death by being given a bowl of water to drink or having its head pushed down so that it seems to be bowed.

in a joyful leap high in the air.
Your brother wins the crown,
a victory surpassing those on the banks
of Alpheus. But sing
a song of victory while I dance.

ELECTRA:
Daylight, gleam of the sun's chariot,
Earth and Night, which I saw before,
now my eyes are free to open wide
since Father's killer Aegisthus has fallen.
Come, let me bring whatever I have,
whatever is stored in the house
to adorn his hair, friends,
so I may crown the head of my victorious brother.

CHORUS:

[Antistrophe]

Bring garlands for his head
while our dance, the Muses' joy,
goes on and on,
now that the kings we loved in times gone by
have overthrown the usurpers
and will rule the land in justice.
Now raise the shout in gladness to the music of the pipe.

(Enter Orestes, Pylades, and servants stage left from the highway, carrying the body of Aegisthus.)

Fourth Episode

ELECTRA: *(To Orestes, as she puts garlands on his head.)*
Glorious in victory, born of a father
victorious in the war at Troy, Orestes,
take this garland for your curls.
You have come home, not after running
a useless footrace, but from killing our enemy
Aegisthus, who killed your father and mine.

864: The site of the ancient Olympics.

And you, too, his companion in arms, son of a most loyal man,
Pylades, take this crown from my hand.
You shared equally with him in the contest.
I wish you happiness and prosperity.

ORESTES:
First, Electra, believe the gods are authors
of this good fortune and then praise me
as a servant of the gods and of luck.
Yes, I have come back from killing Aegisthus
not in word, but in deed; to add
to your certain knowledge of this, I bring you his dead body,
and if you so desire, make him prey for wild beasts
or fix him on a stake for birds to scavenge,
children of the sky. Now he is your slave,
who before was called your master.

ELECTRA:
I am ashamed, though I do want to speak.

ORESTES:
What is it? Go ahead and speak. You have nothing to fear.

ELECTRA:
I'm reluctant to insult the dead for fear of animosity.

ORESTES:
There is nobody who would find fault with you.

ELECTRA:
Our city is hard to please and quick to blame.

ORESTES:
Have your say, sister, if you desire. We were engaged
with him in a hatred that could make no truce.

ELECTRA:
Very well. Where start the tale of woes
and where end it? What words go in the middle?
Every day before dawn I never left off
rehearsing what I wished I could say to your face
if ever I could be free of the old fears.
Now at last I am free. I can even the score,
abusing you as I wanted to when you were alive.
You ruined my life. You made me and my brother

fatherless orphans when we had done you no wrong.
You entered an illicit union with Mother after you killed her husband,
commander of the Greeks, when you never even went to Troy.
And you reached such a depth of lunacy that you expected
you would not get an evil wife when you married my mother,
even after the two of you had fouled my father's bed.
You can be sure of this: when a man corrupts another's wife
in a secret liaison and then has the chance to marry her,
he is a fool if he thinks that when she was
unfaithful to the first she will be faithful to him.
You didn't see it, but your life was miserable.
You knew you had made a sinful marriage, and in you
my mother knew she had acquired a godless husband.
United in evil you shared each other's fate,
you her depravity and she yours.
This is what everybody in Argos was saying about you:
"He belongs to his wife, not she to her husband."
It's a disgrace, for the woman, not the man,
to be head of the household. And the children—
not called after their father's name
but their mother's—I have no respect for them.
When a man marries his better,
he loses his reputation; it's all about the woman.
And this is what deceived you most—though you were oblivious—
you prided yourself in *being* somebody because of your wealth,
which is nothing but a passing acquaintance.
It is nature, not property, that is steady.
Nature stays with you forever and relieves your troubles.
But wealth is unjust and keeps fools for company,
and after blossoming a day or two it is gone in the wind.
Your relations with women—not a proper topic for a virgin—
I will not speak of it, but will put it as a riddle.
You had your way because you ruled the royal roost
and were endowed with good looks. I hope I never have a husband
with a face like a girl, but one with a manly character:
their children grow up to be like Ares;

but the handsome ones only adorn the dance floor.
To hell with you. Time has found you out; you have paid up
but never learned—here is a lesson for a criminal:
even if he runs the first lap without a misstep
he should not think he has overtaken justice until he reaches
the finish line and rounds the final goal of life.

CHORUS:
He has done awful things and paid an awful price
to you and your brother. Justice has proved stronger.

ELECTRA:
So far so good. Now we must carry his body inside
and consign it to darkness, so when Mother
arrives she will not see him dead before her throat is cut.

ORESTES:
Wait. Let's turn to a different story.

ELECTRA: *(Looking off down the road.)*
What's this? Do I see a rescue party from Mycenae?

ORESTES:
No, but my mother who gave me life.

ELECTRA:
Perfect timing then. She is coming straight into the snare.
She really is magnificent in her carriage with all the trappings.

ORESTES:
What do we do about Mother? Are we going to kill her?

ELECTRA:
Has pity come over you because you see your mother in person?

ORESTES:
Woe!
How can I kill her? She gave me life and brought me up.

ELECTRA:
The same way she killed your father and mine.

ORESTES:
Phoebus! Your prophecy shows a total lack of wisdom.

968: "Woe!"—another use of *pheu*. See note on 244.

ELECTRA:
If Apollo is a fool, who are the wise?

ORESTES:
Who decreed that I kill my mother, which I must not do.

ELECTRA:
How can you be tainted if you avenge your father?

ORESTES:
I will have to stand trial for matricide. Before this, I was free of guilt.

ELECTRA:
And yet if you do not vindicate your father you are guilty of impiety.

ORESTES:
But my mother—how will I atone?

ELECTRA:
And what if you fail to appease your father?

ORESTES:
Did an avenging demon speak in the guise of the god?

ELECTRA:
Sitting on Apollo's sacred tripod? I don't think so.

ORESTES:
I cannot believe that was a true prophecy.

ELECTRA:
You must not lose heart and turn into a coward.

ORESTES:
Will I treat her with the same treachery?

ELECTRA:
Yes, the same as when you killed Aegisthus.

976: See Aeschylus' *Libation Bearers* 269–96 for what happens to a man who does not avenge his father's murder.

980: "Apollo's sacred tripod"—The priestess of Apollo (the Pythia) delivered her prophecies seated on a tripod, a three-legged stand or altar.

ORESTES:
I will go in. I am about to begin a terrible business,
and I will do terrible things. If it is the gods' will
so be it, but the ordeal is at once bitter and sweet.

(Exit Orestes into the house.)

CHORUS: *(Addressing Clytemnestra as she arrives stage left from the highway in a carriage attended by two or more Trojan women and driven or led by male attendants.)*

Hail!
Royal lady of the Argive country,
Tyndareos' daughter,
sister of the two noble sons of Zeus,
who live among the stars
in the bright fire of the sky and hold the privilege
of rescuing mortals on heavy seas.
Greetings. I bow to you as to the blessed ones
for your vast wealth and happiness.
Now is the time to look
to your fortunes. Hail, my queen.

CLYTEMNESTRA:
Climb down from the carriage, Trojan women.
Take my hand to help me step down.
The houses of the gods are decked out with Phrygian spoils,
and these women chosen from the Trojan land are my share
in place of my daughter who was taken from me,
a small trophy, but they add to the grace of my house.

ELECTRA:
Am I not a slave, too, cast out of my father's house
to dwell here in poverty—Mother,
may I not take your blessed hand?

CLYTEMNESTRA:
My slaves are here. Do not trouble yourself.

ELECTRA:
You sent me like a captive slave from my home,
and with my home captured I am captured
like these women, left without a father.

CLYTEMNESTRA:
That was your father's doing when he made
the decision to harm those dearest to him.
I will have my say, and yet when a bad reputation
possesses a woman, there is bitterness in her mouth,
not a good thing. I speak from experience. If you understand
the facts, you have the right to hate her, if she is
deserving of hatred. Otherwise, why the hostility?
Tyndareos gave me in marriage to your father
not so that I or the children I bore him would be killed.
Then Agamemnon, after enticing my daughter
with a promise of marriage to Achilles, took her away
to Aulis where the ships were drawn up. And there
he hoisted her over the altar
and cut through Iphigone's white cheek.
If it had been to avert the capture of the city or to benefit his house
or to save our other children that he had to kill one
for the good of many, there might have been an excuse.
But, in fact, because Helen was a wild thing and her husband
didn't know how to control his straying wife—
for that he killed my daughter.
I was aggrieved over losing her, but still
I did not turn savage and kill my husband at once.
But he came home with that god-possessed madwoman
and introduced her into our bed and we were installed
together, two brides in the same house.
We women are giddy creatures, I can't deny it,
but—that being the case—when the husband strays
and pushes away his wife, the woman is likely
to imitate her husband and take on another "friend."
Then blame puts the spotlight on us,
but the responsible party keeps his sterling reputation.
If Menelaus had been carried off from his house in secret,
would I have had to kill Orestes to rescue
my sister's husband? How would your father

1015–17: Compare to Euripides, *Medea* 219–21, 292–305.

1024: Iphigone—alternate form of Iphigenia.

1032: "That god-possessed madwoman"—Cassandra, the captive priestess and prophetess.

have put up with that? Was it right that I suffer
at his hands but he not die for killing my child?
Yes, I killed him. I turned, where I found a way,
to his enemies. Do you think any of your father's friends
would have abetted me in his murder?
It's your turn to speak if you wish and respond freely.
Tell me, if you can, how your father's death was undeserved.

CHORUS:
What you say is just, but it's a disgraceful kind of justice.
A woman must go along with her husband in everything
if she is sensible. Whoever does not agree with this
does not count in my book.

ELECTRA:
Remember, Mother, that your last words
gave me the right to speak freely.

CLYTEMNESTRA:
Yes, and I say it again and I won't take it back.

ELECTRA:
When you hear what I have to say, will you hurt me?

CLYTEMNESTRA:
No. I promise not to. Set your mind at rest.

ELECTRA:
I can speak, then. This is what I have to say first.
Mother, if only you had better sense.
Your good looks do you credit,
Helen's and yours both, but you were born alike,
both vain and unworthy of Castor.
She was "raped" of her own free will and ruined herself,
and you destroyed the best man in all Greece,
holding out the pretext that it was because of your daughter
that you killed your husband. They don't know you as well as I do.
Before your daughter's sacrifice was authorized,
as soon as your husband was out the door
you started arranging your hair in the mirror.
When the man is away from home, if a woman starts
making herself pretty, write her off as a whore.
She has no reason to show her beautiful face

outside the house unless she is looking for trouble.
I'm the only one in all Greece who knows what you are:
if the Trojan side was doing well, you were all smiles
and if it went badly, then your face clouded over
because you did not want Agamemnon to come home from Troy.
And yet you had every opportunity to be virtuous:
you had a husband no worse than Aegisthus,
chosen by all of Greece to be commander in chief;
and when your sister Helen did what she did,
it was possible for you to attain an excellent reputation.
Badness provides an example to do the right thing for all to see.
But if, as you claim, my father killed your daughter,
what harm did my brother or I do you?
How is it that after you killed your husband you did not attach us
more closely to our father's house, but instead brought to your marriage
what didn't belong to you, adding our inheritance to your dowry?
And why is your husband not in exile for your son
or why is he not dead for me, since he killed me twice as much
as my sister even if I am still alive? And if in repayment
for murder there will be more murder, am I to kill you
with the help of your son Orestes, to avenge our father?
If what you did is right, that is right, too.
[Anyone who marries a bad woman for money
instead of nobility is a fool. Poor but virtuous
marriages are better for the home than great ones.]

CHORUS:
[Women's marriages are a matter of luck;
I have seen some turn out well, others badly.]

1097–99: These lines seem to be added to make sense of the chorus' two lines that follow, and are probably an editor's interpolation.

1100–1: The chorus usually speaks between the speeches in an *agōn* (debate) scene to mark off the different speakers. Choruses like to make general remarks that are not necessarily very significant—or even relevant—to what the actors are saying.

CLYTEMNESTRA:
My dear girl, naturally you love your father.
This happens. Some children favor the male parent
and others love their mothers more than their fathers.
I understand. And I'm not really
very happy with what I did, dear child.
But why are you so unwashed and ill-clothed
when you have just given birth?
I regret some of my decisions, especially that
I drove my husband to anger more than I needed to.

ELECTRA:
It's too late for regret when there is no remedy.
Father is dead, but why don't you bring home
your son from his life of exile far from his homeland?

CLYTEMNESTRA:
I'm afraid. I have to look out for my own welfare, not his.
They say he is angry over the murder of his father.

ELECTRA:
Why do you keep your husband so savage against us?

1107–8: Some editors move 1107–8 to open the speech that begins at 1132 because these lines interrupt the flow of Clytemnestra's remarks. In defense of keeping them here, she has just called Electra *teknon* ("my child"), and now takes a real look at her. The sight of Electra's sorry state makes Clytemnestra feel regret more poignantly.

1110: This is a difficult line: the manuscripts have *posin* (accusative of the Greek word for "husband"), which in this context would refer to Aegisthus. With this reading, Clytemnestra regrets egging him on and encouraging his mistreatment of her children from her first marriage (see 1107–8 and 1116). An objection to this is that earlier, the Farmer said she protected them (27–28). Clytemnestra might also refer to her urging Aegisthus' participation in the murder of Agamemnon. The dative *posei,* referring to Agamemnon, has been suggested, and is accepted in many editions and translations. It would mean something like: "that I whipped up my anger excessively against my husband" or "I drove [myself] into anger at my husband." A degree of ambiguity could be maintained by translating "I whipped up anger against my husband more than I should." Clytemnestra regrets nursing and goading anger (her own and Aegisthus') against Agamemnon. This would suggest that she almost cannot remember why she killed him. What is interesting is that the two arguments begin to blend together, as do the two husbands.

CLYTEMNESTRA:
That's his nature, but you are stubborn, too.

ELECTRA:
I am grieving, but I'll put an end to my rage.

CLYTEMNESTRA:
Then he will not be so hard on you.

ELECTRA:
He has proud thoughts. He is in my house.

CLYTEMNESTRA:
There you go. You are igniting new rancor.

ELECTRA:
I'll be silent. I fear him as I fear him.

CLYTEMNESTRA:
Let's stop this talk. Why did you summon me, daughter?

ELECTRA:
You have heard of my miserable childbearing:
help me sacrifice for it—I don't know how—
at the tenth moon, as is customary for a birth.
I have no experience, since this is my first child.

CLYTEMNESTRA:
That's not my job, but the woman who delivered you.

ELECTRA:
I delivered myself and gave birth all alone.

CLYTEMNESTRA:
Is your house so remote and far from friends?

ELECTRA:
No one wants to be friends with the poor.

CLYTEMNESTRA:
Very well. I will go in and sacrifice to the gods
for the completion of the infant's term, and after I do this for you
I must go to the farm where my husband is sacrificing
to the Nymphs. You, servants, take the beasts
and put them to their mangers. Be ready when you think
I have finished this sacrifice to the gods.

(Servants lead away the animals and carriage stage right.)

I have to be there for my husband, too.

(Exit Clytemnestra through the central doors.)

ELECTRA:

Go now inside my impoverished home. But, please, watch out
not to soil your dress on my sooty walls.
You will sacrifice as you must to the gods.
The basket is ready for beginning the ritual and the knife is sharpened
which took down the bull. You will fall, struck down
beside him, and be his bride in Hades' halls,
the man you slept with in life. That favor
I will give you. And you will pay for Father's death.

(Exit Electra through the central doors.)

Third Stasimon

CHORUS:

[Strophe]

Requital of evils—breezes blow
in reverse on the house. Then, in the bath
our leader fell dead:
a loud scream from the house and from the stone copings
when he cried out, "Hard woman, why do you kill me
when I come back to my homeland in the tenth seed time?"
. . . . . .
. . . . . .

[Antistrophe]

Time turning back brings her to justice
for her illicit bed; with her own hand
she killed her husband coming home at last

1140: "My sooty walls"—an allusion to Aeschylus' *Agamemnon* 773–74, "Justice shines her light / on humble, smoke-filled homes." Not even there, as the displacement of the setting tells us: any hut or hovel can serve as the *skēnē* and become the scene of brutal, unseen murder.

1154: Two lines are missing here, the metrical match for 1163–64.

to the high Cyclopean walls
with the sharp blade, taking the axe in her hands.
O suffering
husband, what evil took hold of the wretched woman?
A mountain lioness dwelling in the woods
by the meadowlands brought this about.

CLYTEMNESTRA: *(From within.)*
Children, in the name of the gods, do not kill your mother.

CHORUS:
Do you hear her cry from inside?

CLYTEMNESTRA:
Oh my god!

CHORUS:
I cry out for her, too, as she is overpowered by her children.
A god, you know, metes out justice, whenever it happens.
You suffered harshly. You committed atrocities,
wretched woman, against your husband.

(Enter Electra and Orestes with the dead bodies through the central doors on the ekkyklēma.*)*

Exodos

Kommos

CHORUS:
Look, here they are, coming out, soaked
in the fresh blood of their mother,
evidence of her defeat, the meaning of her miserable cries.
There is no house more unhappy than that
of Tantalus' descendants, and there never has been.

1158: "High Cyclopean walls"—The massive stone architecture in and around Mycenae was attributed to the Cyclopes, one-eyed giants, sons of Uranus and Gaia.

Ekkyklēma: The *ekkyklēma* (thing rolled out) was a revolve or platform on wheels, used to display the result of interior action.

Kommos: A lament sung by chorus and actors.

ORESTES:
Earth and Zeus, who see all
of mortals' affairs, look on these deeds, murderous
and foul, the two bodies lying
together on the ground, struck
by my own hand in vengeance for my loss.

ELECTRA:
So sad, so sad, and I am the cause.
Through fire I plunged against my mother, in my misery,
my mother who gave me life, her daughter.

CHORUS:
Bad luck, it was your bad luck,
mother who bore unforgettable
miseries, unforgettable and worse,
suffering at the hands of your children,
justly you paid for their father's death.

ORESTES:
Phoebus, you intoned your justice
obscurely, but clear are the sorrows
you caused and you bestowed on me,
the murderer's sentence of exile from the land of Hellas.
What other city can I go to?
What stranger, what decent man
will look me in the face,
the man who killed his mother?

ELECTRA:
Woe, woe. Where will I go,
to what choral rites, what marriage?
What husband will take me into his bridal bed?

CHORUS:
Again, your thinking
has shifted again with the wind.
Now your mind is right, but then
it was not, and you did terrible things,
dear girl, to your brother against his will.

ORESTES:
You saw how the poor woman opened
her gown, bared her breast as she was being murdered.

Woe. She let the limbs that gave me birth
fall to the ground, and her hair—I—

CHORUS:
I see clearly how you passed through torment
when you heard the heart-rending moan
of the mother who gave you life.

ORESTES:
These words she screamed as she stretched out her hand
to my face: "My child, I beg you."
She hung from my cheek
so the weapon fell from my hand.

CHORUS:
The unhappy one, how did you dare to look
with your own eyes on the murder of your mother
as she breathed her last?

ORESTES:
I held my cloak over my eyes
and began the sacrifice, letting the knife
go into my mother's neck.

ELECTRA:
And I urged you on.
I put my hand on the weapon with yours.

CHORUS:
You have caused the most terrible of sufferings.

1208–9: "She let the limbs . . . and her hair"—Orestes cannot finish the line (an example of *aposiopesis,* an abrupt breaking off in the midst of a phrase). During the murder, when Clytemnestra dropped to the floor, he would have taken hold of her hair—the only part of her he would have had to touch—as he pulled her head back to slit her throat. He would have leaned over her and she reached up to touch his cheek (1216). According to another reading of 1209, Orestes says, "I felt faint."

1221: "I held my cloak over my eyes"—Like Perseus beheading the Gorgon, Orestes covers his eyes.

1225: Besides having the most vivid description (in the form of a reenactment) of the murder of Clytemnestra, this is the only version in which Electra is physically present and takes part.

ORESTES:
Take hold, cover Mother's limbs with her robe
and fit back her slit throat.
You gave birth to us, your own murderers.

ELECTRA:
Look, we are putting your robes around you,
Mother, loved and unloved.

Dei ex Machina

(The Dioscuri appear above the rooftop on the mēchanē.*)*

CHORUS:
This is the end of great evils for the house.
But, look! Here on top of the building
there are appearing some divinities or some of
the heavenly gods. This is not the way
mortals approach. Why in the world are they coming
into the clear sight of men?

DIOSCURI (CASTOR speaking):
Son of Agamemnon, listen. Your mother's
two brothers address you, the sons of Zeus:
I am Castor, and this is my brother Polydeuces.
Just now we have put down the violent disturbance
of a ship at sea and arrived in Argos when we saw
the murder of our sister here, your mother.
She has met with justice but you did not do justice,
and Phoebus—Phoebus is my king;
I will hold my tongue—he is wise, but his oracle was not.
Still we must go along with it. It is necessary now
to do what Fate and Zeus have decreed about you.
To Pylades give Electra to take home as his wife.
And you—leave Argos. You are not permitted
to walk in the city after killing your mother.
The terrible fates, the dog-faced goddesses,
will drive you wandering in madness.
When you reach Athens, embrace the holy statue

Mēchanē: The *mēchanē* (machine) was a crane that lifted actors above the scene building.

1252: "The dog-faced goddesses"—the Erinyes or Furies.

of Pallas Athena. As they swarm you with their hissing snakes,
she will keep them off, so they cannot touch you,
raising over your head the circle of the Gorgon's face.
There is the Rock of Ares where the gods first sat
to pass judgment in a case of murder
when brutal Ares killed Halirrhothius
son of the lord of the sea in anger
over his daughter's ungodly coupling, where a vote
most sacred in the eyes of the gods is secure from that time.
There you must risk trial for murder.
Equal votes cast will save you from
the penalty of death. Loxias will take the blame
upon himself for commanding the murder of your mother.
And this law will be established for all time
that the defendant always wins when the votes are equal.
And the dreaded goddesses overcome by this distress
will go down into a cleft of the earth right beside the hill,
which will be a solemn holy oracle for mankind.
You must go to live in a city of the Arcadians
by the streams of Alpheus near the sacred Lycian precinct;
the city will be named after you.
This much I have to say to you. Aegisthus' body
will be given a proper burial by the citizens of Argos.

1259: "The Rock of Ares"—the Areopagus (Ares' hill or outcrop), the Athenians' homicide court, northwest of the Acropolis in Athens. Euripides attributes the founding of the court of the Areopagus to the gods' trial of Ares for killing Poseidon's son Halirrhothius, who had raped Ares' daughter. Aeschylus, *The Furies* (*Eumenides*) 481–84 represents Athena establishing the court for Orestes' trial.

1265–66: "Equal votes cast will save you"—See Aeschylus, *The Furies* (*Eumenides*) 735, 741, 752–53, on the vote of Athena, which favors the defendant in the event of a tie.

1271: "Cleft of the earth"—See Aeschylus, *The Furies* (*Eumenides*) 805; the cleft or chasm is at the northeast angle of the Areopagus.

1273–75: "You must go . . . the city will be named after you"—In other versions, Orestes is only temporarily exiled and returns to rule in Mycenae. The city dubiously named for him is Orestheion (mentioned in Thucydides, *The Peloponnesian War* 5.64.3 and Herodotus, *The Histories* 9.11), near the source of the Alpheus River. The Lycian sanctuary of Zeus is on Mount Lykaion, a mountain in Arcadia in the west central Peloponnesus, about twenty-two miles from Olympia (see map).

But as for your mother—Menelaus—he's just arrived
in Nauplia from the time he captured Troy—
he and Helen will bury her. Helen has come
from the house of Proteus in Egypt and did not go to Troy.
To cause strife and death among mortals, Zeus
sent a phantom of Helen to Troy.
Let Pylades take his bride and go home
to Achaean country, and let him take along
that man called your brother-in-law
into the land of the Phocians and give him a mass of wealth.
You now, set out over the neck of the isthmus
and go to the prosperous hill of Cecrops.
For after completing your appointed sentence for murder
you will prosper, free of troubles.

ORESTES:
Sons of Zeus, may we approach
and speak with you?

CASTOR:
Yes, you are not polluted by these slaughters.

ELECTRA:
May I be part of the dialogue, too, sons of Tyndareos?

CASTOR:
Yes, you, too. I attribute this act
of murder to Phoebus.

ORESTES:
How is it that though you are gods
and the brothers of the murdered woman
you did not hold off the Furies from the house?

1276–80: In Homer's *Odyssey* (3.309–10), Orestes himself gives the funeral feast—of both Aegisthus and his mother—for the Argives.

1280–81: The story of Helen in Egypt appears in Herodotus' *Histories*, Stesichorus' Palinode (quoted in Plato, *Phaedrus* 243a–b), and the *Cypria*, as well as in Homer's *Odyssey.*

1283: "Phantom of Helen"—The reunion of the real Helen and Menelaus in Egypt after the Trojan War is the subject of Euripides' *Helen.*

1289: Cecrops—a mythical king of Athens.

1292ff.: The distribution of lines is uncertain.

CASTOR:
Fate's grim necessity led to what had to be
and the commands of Phoebus, less than wise.

ELECTRA:
What Apollo, what oracles decreed
that I become Mother's murderer?

CASTOR:
Shared actions, shared fates;
one madness of your fathers
tears through you both.

ORESTES:
My sister, seeing you after so long,
I am to lose the joy of your love so soon,
and when I leave I will leave you behind.

CASTOR:
She has a husband and home. She has not
suffered brutally, except that she is leaving
the city of Argos.

ELECTRA:
And what other grief is greater
than to leave the borders of your homeland?

ORESTES:
And I will go away from my father's home
and submit Mother's murder
to the votes of aliens.

CASTOR:
Be brave. You will go
to the holy city of Pallas. Have courage.

ELECTRA:
Press your breast to mine,
dearest brother.
The curses of Mother's murder
sever us from our father's home.

ORESTES:
Throw yourself into my arms. Embrace me. Raise the dirge
as you would at my tomb if I were dead.

CASTOR:
Alas, alas. Your cries of grief are terrible
even for gods to hear.
There is in me and the heavenly gods
pity for mortals full of suffering.

ORESTES:
I will not see you again.

ELECTRA:
And I will not come again into your sight.

ORESTES:
This is the last time you will speak to me.

ELECTRA:
Farewell, city.
A long farewell to you, fellow women of the city.

ORESTES:
Most loyal—are you going now?

ELECTRA:
I am going. My face is wet with tears.

(Exit Electra and Pylades stage left.)

ORESTES:
Pylades, good-bye.
Make my sister your bride.

(Exit Orestes, running, stage right.)

CASTOR:
Marriage will be their care. The dogs are here!
Run from them now, racing to Athens.
They will set upon you a frightening pace,
snake-handed, black-coated,
bearing fruit of terrible pains.
We two must leave in haste, soaring
through stretches of the sky to the Sikel sea
to rescue the seafaring ships.
We do not come to the aid of the polluted
but those who hold what's right, holy, and dear

1348: Sikel—the sea between Sicily and Greece (see map).

in life; releasing them
from hard toils, we keep them safe.
Let no one choose to be unjust;
let no one side with perjurers.
As a god, I have this to say to mortals.

(Exit the Dioscuri on the mēchanē.*)*

CHORUS:
Farewell! If anyone can fare well
and not be broken by bad luck,
he alone will prosper.

(The chorus files out in both directions.)

–END–

SOPHOCLES

Electra

Translated with Notes by Paul Woodruff

Cast of Characters

TUTOR	an old man who raised Orestes away from home
ORESTES	younger brother of Electra
ELECTRA	daughter of Agamemnon who has grown past the age of marriage
CHORUS	of women of Mycenae
CHRYSÓTHEMIS	Electra's sister, also unmarried
CLYTEMNESTRA	Agamemnon's widow; mother of Electra, Chrysóthemis, and Orestes
AEGISTHUS	Clytemnestra's lover and second husband, partner in the murder of Agamemnon
	Nonspeaking Roles
PYLADES	Orestes' close friend
ATTENDANTS	to Clytemnestra

Sophocles' *Electra*

SCENE: *The front of the royal house at Mycenae, where Agamemnon used to rule, with two great doors in the center of the set. Near the doors, in front of the house, stands a statue of Apollo. The time is about ten years after the murder of Electra's father, Agamemnon, by Clytemnestra and her lover Aegisthus.*

(Enter the Tutor, Orestes, and Pylades through the stage left wing. They stand some distance from the great doors. Orestes has reached military age, about twenty years old.)

TUTOR:

My boy, your father commanded the army at Troy.
You are Agamemnon's son. And now you are here at last
To see for yourself, as you always wanted to do,
This place, this legend-haunted, longed-for land of Argos.
Io was driven across this plain by stinging flies.
And over there, Orestes, Apollo Wolf-slayer
Gave his name to the agora. That place on the left
Is Hera's famous temple. Where we stand now,
You may say you are looking at gold-rich Mycenae.

(Pointing to the great doors.)

4: "Land of Argos"—the land of which Mycenae was the capital during the time depicted in Homer's epics, the same time depicted in the play. In myth, Io was transformed into a cow and driven across this plain. Argos was also the name of the capital city at the time the play was written. It was known for its agora, a public market area dedicated to Apollo, and for its temple to Hera.

6: Apollo—the presiding deity of this play. For his place in earlier versions of the story, see Introduction, pp. xiii, xvi, and xxvi. His epithet *Lykeios* could refer to his special affinity for light ("Lord of Light") or to some connection with wolves, probably through his role as protector of sheep from wolves ("Wolfish"). Here Sophocles refers to the myth of wolf-slaying that gave the agora at Argos its name. See 645 and 1379. Other versions of the story tell us that Orestes carries out Apollo's will in killing his mother. Sophocles' version leaves this an open question. See note on 35–38.

And this blood-drenched house belongs to the family
Of Pelops. I carried you away from your father's murder,
Away from this place, when your own blood sister
Gave you to me, so that I could save your life,
Bring you up to young manhood, and train you
To be the avenger of your father's death. Now, therefore,
Orestes, and you too, Pylades, dearest friend,
We must decide quickly what to do. The sun's rays,
As you see, are already raising the voices of birds,
And stars are fading from the dark and kindly skies.
So before the first man ventures from this house,
We'd better say enough to settle a plan. We mustn't shrink
Or hesitate a moment longer. Now is the time to act.

ORESTES:

You are very near my heart, more than any other serving man.
You've proved your nobility to me many times.
You are like a well-bred horse: Even when it's old,
A fine horse shows spirit at terrible threats
And pricks up its ears. That's the way
You spur me on and follow in the front rank.
Now I'll reveal my secret plans to you.
You must keep a sharp ear to what I say,
And if I miss my target, you must set me right.
You know I went to the Pythian Oracle at Delphi
To find out what strategy would make
My father's murderers pay the price for what they did.
Apollo answered my questions along these lines:
By myself, without mustering an armed force,

11: Pelops—See note on 505 for the tale of the curse on Pelops. See also House of Pelops Family Tree.

16: Pylades—Orestes' friend. In this play he has no lines, but he is always present with Orestes, and he presumably helps in the killing that will take place.

32: Pythia—the priestess who spoke for Apollo as the oracle at Delphi.

35–38: The text is unclear about whether the god himself endorses the action that Orestes will take. Orestes has not asked whether he should kill the guilty pair, but rather how he can make them pay the price, and Orestes here has rephrased the oracle's answer in his own words. The expression "they deserve" may or may not come directly from Apollo. Both sides pray to Apollo, Clytemnestra at 637–59 and Electra at 1376–83. As Electra approaches the deed, she still feels the need to make sure that Apollo is on her side.

To trick them, sneak in, and, with my own hand, do
The slaughter they deserve. So on this basis,
You are to go and, when the right moment strikes you,
Enter this house and find out everything they are doing,
So that you can give me a report from firsthand knowledge.
Your old age and the passing of many years will keep you
From being recognized. They won't suspect a thing.
Tell them this story: You are a visitor who's come
From Phocis, and you represent Phanoteus,
Who happens to be their biggest ally.
Give them this message under oath:
Orestes died in a fatal accident.
When he was chariot racing at the Pythian Games,
He was thrown from his perch. That's your story.
As for us, we'll go first to Father's tomb, as the god directed,
To make a libation, and I'll cut a fine bunch of hair
To crown his grave. Then we'll come back here again,
Carrying in our hands the bronze urn—
You know, the one we hid in the bushes—
So that we can sneak in with a phony tale
That will delight them. We'll say that my remains
Are already burned and reduced to ashes.
How could this hurt me? I'll be dead, according to what I say,
But what I do will make me safe—and famous.
In my opinion, if a statement gives you an advantage,
It's never bad. I've known many clever men
Who were falsely reported dead. Then, when they came
Back home, their reputation was higher than ever.
So it is for me: I proclaim that through this message
I shall strike the eyes of my enemies like a flaming star.

39: "The right moment"—*kairos,* a term that will have a major role in this text. See 76, "good timing."

45: Phocis—the land where Orestes grew up in safety, not far from Delphi, where his host was Strophius. (See map.) Strophius had a long-standing feud with his twin brother, beginning before they were born when they fought in their mother's womb. Phanoteus (or Panopeus in Homer) is the son of Strophius' brother; as the hereditary enemy of Orestes' host, he is a friend and ally of Clytemnestra and Aegisthus.

49: Pythian Games—games that were held at Delphi, where ruins of the stadium remain to this day. The events were similar to those of the Olympian Games; in both, the greatest glory was attached to the chariot race.

And now, land of my father, gods of this place,
Receive me on this successful journey of mine.
And you,

(Turning to the great doors.)

home of my father, I have come with justice
On a mission from the gods to scrub out the stain.
Do not reject me from this land in disgrace.
Give me mastery of my wealth and power to bring order
To my house. That is what I have to say.

Now, old man, go and look after your assigned job.
We two will leave. The time is ripe, and when men act,
They are governed above all by good timing.

ELECTRA: *(With a cry offstage.)*
I am so miserable!

TUTOR:
Listen, child. I think I heard one of the maidservants
Crying inside the house.

(Enter Electra through the great doors. She stands at center stage.)

ORESTES:
Is this Electra? Poor thing! What do you want to do?
Should we stay and listen to her grief?

TUTOR:
Certainly not. Nothing before Apollo's command;
We must set out to follow that as our guide
And make the libation to your father. This leads
To victory, I assure you, and power over the perpetrators.

(Exit the Tutor, followed by Orestes and Pylades, through the stage right wing.)

77: The stage direction "*With a cry*" marks an expression of grief in the Greek. The ancient text gives no stage directions, but it frequently includes expressions of grief that are not translatable into English, which does not have resources for expressing emotion that are as credible as those in ancient Greek. With this stage direction, which recurs throughout the text, actors may groan or cry appropriately.

85: "Power over the perpetrators"—in an alternative translation, "power in our actions." The Greek wording is ambiguous.

ELECTRA:

O holy light!
O air, earth's equal partner!
How many cries of grief have you heard?
How many times have you seen me
Draw blood as I beat at my breast
When black night lifted?
O these all-night festivals of weeping!
That loathsome bed at home—
How well I know every lump in it, lying awake,
Mourning for my poor father.
He could have been an honored guest in a foreign grave
If the bloody war had taken him.

But no. My mother and her playmate in bed,
Aegisthus, like a pair of lumberjacks
At an oak tree, took a bloody axe and split his skull.
Now, O my father, no one weeps for you but me.
I am the only one who cries out against your murder.
And I will never stop.
I will shout my sadness to the world,
So long as shining stars plunge around the sky
Or sunlight beams into my eyes.
Like the nightingale who sings
For her murdered child, I will proclaim
My raging grief to everyone
In front of these, my father's gates.

I call on hell, home of Hades and Persephone;
I call Hermes out of the dark earth

107: "The nightingale"—According to legend, Procne was transformed into a nightingale after killing her child Itys in an act of revenge against Itys' father. As a bird, she sings mournfully, "Itys, Itys" (148). An ambiguity in the Greek allows us to read, with Jebb (1894), "the nightingale, slayer of her offspring," but I agree with Kells (1973) that Electra here alludes simply to grief for a murdered child, leaving open the issue of responsibility.

111–14: Hades and Persephone preside over the Underworld, where the dead live. Hermes is the messenger god who guides the dead to Hades and may also serve as a guide to those who avenge the dead. Ara is the personification of the curse Agamemnon presumably called down on his killers. The Furies (Erinyes) are deities of vengeance who pursue killers.

And Ara, Mistress of the Curse;
I call the god-begotten holy Furies—
You who witness every murder,
You who watch adulterous thieves of sex—
Come, you gods! Be my army!
Punish those who killed my father,
And bring my brother to me!
I am alone; pain presses me down;
I do not have the strength to stand against it any longer.

(Enter the chorus through the stage right wing, singing as they take their places in the orchestra.)

Parodos (Entry-song)

[Strophe *a*]

CHORUS:
Dear child, Electra,
Daughter of disaster-mother,
Will you weep and wail forever?
What will be enough for you? To melt in tears?
That's old news now—Agamemnon getting trapped,
Deceived by your mother, utterly godless,
Betrayed by her wicked hand.
And the man behind it all—may I say it aloud?—
I wish he were dead!

ELECTRA:
Dear women,
You are true to your noble birth.
I am in anguish, and you came to comfort me.
Believe me, I understand what you say;
You are not unheard.
But I do not want to give this up—
Ceaseless, raucous mourning for my poor father.
Leave me to my madness!
For the sake of our dear friendship, yours and mine,

121–250: Parodos—the entry-song for the chorus. Here Sophocles breaks with tradition by turning it into a sung debate between Electra and the older women.

(A loud cry of anguish.)

Please go!

[Antistrophe *a*]

CHORUS:
But you—
You'll never raise him up!
Hades sucks everyone down.
Your father needs no tears or prayers from you!
You were right to grieve at first,
But now it's absurd, this endless wailing.
You'll cry yourself to death. Tell me:
Why are you so devoted to your pain?

ELECTRA:
Could anyone forget
The horror of a parent's death?
Or learn to be as silent as a baby?
My mind is stamped in the image of a crying bird,
Who calls for her dead child forever, "Itys, Itys!"
And mindless with grief, she is Zeus' messenger.
O you all-suffering Niobe, I follow you as my goddess
Because you kept on weeping, weeping
While you were transformed into stone,

(A loud cry of anguish.)

And even your rock-tomb wept!

[Strophe *b*]

CHORUS:
But you are not alone, child:

147–48: "Crying bird . . . 'Itys, Itys!'"—The nightingale ushers in spring and, in this way, is a messenger of Zeus. Its cry is heard as one of mourning for its dead child. For the myth, see note on 107.

150: Niobe had offended the goddess Leto by bragging about her human children. Leto's divine offspring, Apollo and Artemis, killed the children to punish Niobe. According to the story, as Niobe wept for her loss, she became a granite surface in the mountains, over which water dripped perpetually, like a woman who never ceases to weep. See Sophocles' *Antigone* 832.

All mortals suffer pain. You let it hurt too much.
The others in your house—
Same father, same blood as you,
Chrysóthemis and Iphianassa—
They live with the same loss as you;
Why do you take it over the edge?
And what about the boy who was hidden from pain?
He is well born and happy, and someday
Mycenae, our famous land, will have him back
At the altar of Zeus, who cares for us. Orestes will come!

ELECTRA:
He's the one I'm waiting for! I never give up.
I hang on—unmarried, childless, fluttering in misery,
Sodden with tears—while my string of bad luck
Runs on and on. But Orestes forgets his pain
And what he knows of mine.
How can he send message after message?
None of them come true!
Always he says, "I long to come! I long to come!"
All right! But then show yourself to me!

[Antistrophe *b*]

CHORUS:
Be hopeful, child, be hopeful.
Even now, in heaven, great Zeus
Sees all, rules all.
Let *him* bear your grief. It is too much for you.
And as for those you hate, do not forget,
But do not hate too much.
Time is a soft and gentle god.

157: Iphianassa—in Homeric legend, the name of one of Agamemnon's daughters. In one surviving version of the story of Agamemnon's human sacrifice, she replaces Iphigenia (whose name was unknown to Homer) as the daughter whose life Agamemnon gave to obtain a fair wind for Troy. Here she is simply another sister of Electra (see House of Pelops Family Tree).

165: "I hang on—unmarried"—Electra's name means "unbedded," that is, "unmarried." Electra's family are afraid that a son of Electra's would seek revenge for his grandfather's death.

And still the lord of the cow-grazed height of Crisa,
Apollo, turns this over and over in his mind.
So does Agamemnon's son.
And so does the godlike king himself, by Acheron.

ELECTRA:
But what about me? What hope can I have?
My life drains away; my strength is gone.
I am some childless woman
With no man to depend on.
I am no better than a foreign servant, a worthless woman,
Brought to tend my father's room,
Dressed in these rags, laying food on a table
That has no place for me.

[Strophe *c*]

CHORUS: *(Remembering the killing of Agamemnon.)*
Agony to hear, a scream at homecoming,
Agony, in the lap of ancestors,
When he faced the bronze jaws,
Startled by their assault.
Deception spoke then, lust had its way,
And what they conceived was horrible, horribly given shape,
Whether it was a human—or a god—
Who made it be.

179: Crisa—a plain, sacred to Apollo, that runs from near Delphi to the sea at the Gulf of Corinth. See map for Crisa's proximity to Phocis, Orestes' place of exile.

182: "The godlike king himself, by Acheron"—Agamemnon. In myth, Acheron is a river in the Underworld. The Greek allows another translation: "the god who is lord by Acheron," i.e., Hades (so Jebb 1894). My translation follows Kells 1973.

195: "The bronze jaws"—the two-bladed axe used in the killing.

199–200: "Whether it was a human . . . made it be"—The chorus refers to the tradition that such events in Agamemnon's family are due to the curse on the house of Pelops, but this in no way weakens their charge against the lovers who killed the king. Sophocles generally assigns responsibility to humans for the choices they make. For example, even when Oedipus acts as fate, oracular prediction, and divine will would have him, Sophocles nevertheless shows Oedipus making choices that lead to the preordained end. See Woodruff 2008, pp. 75–76, for a discussion of choice in *Oedipus at Colonus*.

ELECTRA:

The day I hate beyond all others,
The day of my worst enemies!
The night, festival of anguish,
Unspeakable, when my father saw
His own death, his murder at their hands.
When they caught up my life
And threw it away, ruined.
Great god on Olympus,
Make them pay the full price in pain!
Never let them taste the joy of triumph,
Because they did this thing.

[Antistrophe *c*]

CHORUS:

Tell yourself: "Do not raise your voice again."
Have you any idea where this leads?
You are so far out of line, you'll fall
Blindly into ruin, your own blindness.
You'll get more than your share of trouble
If the sick spirit in your soul
Is pregnant with battle, if it always hatches war.
Never launch a quarrel against the powers that be!

ELECTRA:

But I have to be dreadful in dreadful times. Necessity!
I understand my passions; they are no mystery to me.
But in dreadful times, how could I hold back?
This blind fury seethes
Until I die.
Dear friends, noble as you are, no one now

209: Olympus—in myth, the mountain home of Zeus and his family of gods.

226–27: This line, literally a rhetorical question, has been read in several different ways. The main alternatives are: (1) "For from whom, noble friends, could I hear a word that would be helpful, in the judgment of anyone who thinks right?" (from the Greek in Kells 1973); (2) "For who that thinks right would judge that any word would help me?" (from the Greek in Jebb 1894, Lloyd-Jones 1994). I have adopted a simplified version of the first alternative.

Can tell me anything that helps.
No one with good sense would think otherwise.
Please go away; spare me your comfort.
My pain is beyond cure,
And I will never let it go.
I will weep without end.

[Epode]

CHORUS:
All right, but I meant well.
I spoke like a mother, from my heart:
Trust me! Do not hatch ruin out of ruin!

ELECTRA:
Set limits to evil? Impossible!
How could it be good to neglect the dead?
Would human nature bear it?
Save me from the "honor" of restraint!
And, if I may speak from my heart,
Save me from the peaceful life
That would dishonor my parents
And clip the wings from my shrill soaring cries.
Because my poor father lies dead,
Because he is earth and nothing,
They, in return,
Shall pay the price—death for death—
If any strength remains
In the reverence and respect of mortals.

CHORUS:
As for me, dear child, I came because I care
Deeply for you, as for myself. If I speak wrong,
You win. I will follow you.

ELECTRA:
It shames me, ladies, if you judge
Me guilty of excessive pain and grief.
But be understanding: Violence forces me
To act this way. How could any highborn
Woman see her father's suffering and not act so?
His death is always before my eyes,
Day and night, growing like a healthy weed.

First, my mother's part in this—because she bore me—
Is the cruelest blow of all. And then,
In my own home I rub shoulders with the killers
Of my father. I am at their command; I depend
On them. Sometimes they give me what I need;
Sometimes they don't. And what kind of life
Do you think I can lead? When Aegisthus sits
In front of me on the throne that was my father's,
When he wears Father's clothes and pours libations
For hearth and home right where they killed him—
And I have no choice but to watch all this?
Then the ultimate outrage—I see him,
The murderer himself, in Father's bed
With Mother. "Mother"? That disaster of a woman!
Can I really call her that when she's the bedmate
Of that man? She is so shameless, she sleeps
With pollution, and she does not fear the fury
Of the gods! It's as if she's laughing away her crimes.
She keeps track of the anniversary of the day
She killed my father after tricking him.
And on that day she has a festival
Of sacred dance and sacrifices to the gods,
Gods she thinks will protect her.
Poor me! I watch all this from under the same roof,
Wasting myself with tears, screaming at the horror
Of the feast named for my father.
I cry alone, by myself, with never enough tears
To satisfy the hunger of my angry soul.
And she mocks me: "So! One high-toned woman—only one—
Keeps saying this was wrong. No one else complains
Or calls it hateful to the gods. Are you the first
To have a father die? The only human being
To suffer and to grieve? Devil take you!
I hope the gods below never set you free
From all your weeping and wailing." That's how

275–76: "She sleeps with pollution"—As the killer of Clytemnestra's husband, Aegisthus carries a kind of curse, a pollution that has not been washed away. According to tradition, when a murderer remains in the land of his victim, pollution lies on the land. This idea lies behind the plot of Sophocles' *Oedipus Tyrannus*.

She insults me. But when she hears that Orestes
May be on the way, she comes after me,
Shouting like mad, "It's all your fault! You did it!
You stole Orestes right out of my hands.
Damn sure I'll make you pay for that."
That's how she howls for justice. And he's beside her,
Cheering her on, her famous fresh-made husband,
Totally pathetic, can't do anything on his own,
Has to have a woman fight his battles for him.
So while I keep waiting for Orestes to come
And put a stop to all my trouble, I am perishing here.
And what's Orestes doing? Nothing but having good
Intentions, which are smashing all my hopes,
Both here and there. At times like these, my friends,
It would be crazy to be sane or reverent.
Bad times make bad deeds a necessity.

CHORUS:
Tell me: Is Aegisthus at home? Would you
Say this while he's near? Or is he away?

ELECTRA:
Of course he's away. If he were near,
I'd have stayed indoors. Right now he's in the fields.

CHORUS:
Well then, in that case, I might find
The courage to join in what you say.

ELECTRA:
He's gone all right. What do you want to know?

CHORUS:
Here's my question for you: Your brother—
Is he coming now or later? I want to know.

ELECTRA:
He says he's coming, but he doesn't do what he says.

CHORUS:
Men often hold back when the job is enormous.

ELECTRA:
But I saved his life. And it wasn't by holding back!

CHORUS:
Be hopeful. A noble nature never fails his friends.

ELECTRA:
So I believe. That's what's kept me alive this long.

(Enter Chrysóthemis through the great doors during the following speech.)

CHORUS:
No more words now, nothing. I see your sister
Coming from the house—Chrysóthemis. Like you,
She has her father's nature—and her mother's. Look!
In her hands she has gifts to offer, as custom dictates, to the dead.

CHRYSÓTHEMIS:
What is this noise you're making just outside
Our doorway? Sister, what are you saying?
After so much time, are you still refusing to learn
How silly it is to indulge in empty displays of emotion?
At least I understand the situation I am in:
I am in so much agony over the way things are now.
If I were strong enough, I'd show them what I think of them,
But I have decided that in a storm it's best to slacken sail
And not pretend to take action when you're causing them
No pain. You should follow my example. As for justice,
I agree: I am not speaking up for justice;
Your judgment is correct. Still, I must live in freedom,
And to do that I must totally obey the powers that be.

ELECTRA:
Dreadful! Absurd! Your father's the source of who you are.
Yet you forget him and think only of the woman
Who gave you birth. You learned everything from her.
When you scold me, it comes from her, not you.
Take your pick: Either you are out of your mind,
Or you've stayed sane by putting family out of mind.

327: "Gifts to offer . . . to the dead"—in this case, offerings meant to pacify the angry dead, probably consisting of a pitcher for pouring out fine oil as a libation, flowers, and cakes (so Jebb 1894; see also 433–34).

346: "Family"—*philoi,* "dear ones." In this context it means family and specifically the women's father (so Jebb 1894).

The way you are speaking now, if you were strong,
You'd show how much you hate all this.
But when I demand total vengeance for Father,
You won't act with me. And when I act, you try to stop me.
What is this but cowardice on top of our trouble?
Explain to me—or else take my point—
What would I gain by silencing my grief?
I have my life, don't I? It's bad, but it's enough
For me. And I give pain to *them,* so if there's any joy
Down there, the dead man has some satisfaction.
Yes, you hate, but your hatred is only a word.
Action killed Father, and you're cozy with the killers.
I would never give in to those people—
Even if they promised me all the luxuries
You revel in today. Never! You can have
That gourmet food. Stuff yourself with it.
All the nourishment I need I take by not disappointing
Myself. I don't want any part of the rewards you get,
And you wouldn't either if you were sane. You had a chance
To be known for the excellence of our wonderful father,
And you chose Mother. So most people think you're rotten,
Now that Father's dead, and you've betrayed your own family.

CHORUS:
Not so angry, by the gods! You'd both be better off
If you learned something from each other. You should apply
Her words to your life, and she should apply yours to hers.

CHRYSÓTHEMIS:
As for me, ladies, I have become rather accustomed
To the things she says. I would never have brought it up,
Except that trouble is coming her way on a huge scale,
So I heard. That will stop her endless wailing.

ELECTRA:
Really? Tell me what's so dreadful. If it's worse
Than the trouble I have now, I'll stop arguing.

CHRYSÓTHEMIS:
All right, I'll tell you everything I know.
Their plan is this: If you don't quit this lamentation,
They will send you away to a place where never again
Will you see the light of the sun. You will be alive

Under the roof of a dungeon far from this land, and there
You may sing of your troubles. Think this over, and, later on,
Don't blame me if you suffer. Now is the time to get smart.

ELECTRA:
That is what they plan to do to me?

CHRYSÓTHEMIS:
Absolutely. As soon as Aegisthus comes home.

ELECTRA:
Then I hope he makes it here quickly.

CHRYSÓTHEMIS:
What are you saying? It will haunt you.

ELECTRA:
I want him to come if he has a mind to do any of this.

CHRYSÓTHEMIS:
What are you aiming at? Have you lost your mind?

ELECTRA:
I aim to get as far as I can away from all of you.

CHRYSÓTHEMIS:
Don't you care at all about the life you have now?

ELECTRA:
Yes, it's a fine life I lead. Wonderful.

CHRYSÓTHEMIS:
But it would be—if you'd only learn to think straight.

ELECTRA:
Don't you try to persuade me to turn against family.

CHRYSÓTHEMIS:
I am not trying to persuade you to do anything.
Just give in to the powers that be.

ELECTRA:
You mean suck up to them, like you! I can't live your way!

CHRYSÓTHEMIS:
But good judgment is a fine thing if it keeps you from falling down.

395: "Family"—See note on 346.

ELECTRA:
I'll fall, if I have to, avenging Father.

CHRYSÓTHEMIS:
Father would understand this and forgive.

ELECTRA:
Congratulations on your wisdom! A coward would say the same.

CHRYSÓTHEMIS:
So you're not persuaded? You won't agree with me?

ELECTRA:
No way. I hope I'll never be such an idiot.

CHRYSÓTHEMIS:
Then I will leave you. I was sent out for a purpose.

ELECTRA:
Where *are* you going? These offerings—who are they for?

CHRYSÓTHEMIS:
Mother sent me to pour libations at Father's tomb.

ELECTRA:
What? Though he hates her more than anyone?

CHRYSÓTHEMIS:
Though she killed him. That's what you meant to say.

ELECTRA:
Did she get this idea from some friend? Who is she trying to please?

CHRYSÓTHEMIS:
She got it from fear, because of her dream. That's what I think.

ELECTRA: *(Cheerfully.)*
O gods of our father, be with us now, above all!

CHRYSÓTHEMIS:
Does Mother's panic give you some reason to hope?

ELECTRA:
Tell me what she saw. Then I'll answer.

CHRYSÓTHEMIS:
But I don't know much; I can say only a little.

ELECTRA:
Then tell me that! Often, a few words are enough
To ruin a human life or to save one.

CHRYSÓTHEMIS:
Word is that she saw our father, yours and mine,
And he was living with her again, after he had returned
Into the light. And then, in front of the hearth,
He took and planted his scepter, the one he used to hold,
Which Aegisthus has now, and from it sprang
A vigorous young branch that cast its shade
Over all the land of Mycenae.
I heard these details from someone who was there
When Mother revealed her dream to the Sun.
More than this I do not know. Except:
She sent me out on account of this fear.
Now, I beg you, by the gods of our people, take my advice:
Don't let yourself fall down as a result of bad judgment.
If you push me away now, you'll be back when you're in trouble.

ELECTRA:
No, darling! Those things you are carrying—
Don't let any of them touch his tomb. It would be an outrage,
An irreverence, to bring that hateful woman's gifts
As offerings for Father's grave. No libations, either.
No. Toss them in the wind or dig them a hole
Deep in the earth, where none of them will ever come near
Our father's resting place. *She* can have them when she dies,
Her own little buried treasure, which we saved for her.
First off, if she weren't the hardest-hearted woman on earth,
She'd never send you to honor the man she killed
With a crown of offerings, a libation of hate.
Ask yourself: Do you think the dead man would accept
These gifts as tokens of friendship? When he died

425: "Revealed her dream to the Sun"—Helios, the sun god.

428–30: The manuscripts assign these lines to Electra, but that is impossible. The warning against bad judgment can only come from Chrysóthemis.

At her hand, dishonored, like a worthless enemy?
When she hacked off his legs? Wiped the blood
Off her hands onto his hair? Don't tell me you believe
You could wash her crimes away! Not with the things
You carry. No way! Get rid of them. Do this instead:
Cut off the waving tresses of your hair at the end,
And cut mine, too. It isn't much, but in my sad state,
That's all I have, dull as it is. But give it to him, please,
And take this belt of mine, although it's very plain.
Fall on your knees and make this prayer: "May he rise
From the earth to be our friend and ally, may he strike
Our enemies, and may his son Orestes have the upper hand.
May our enemies learn that he is still alive
When he has crushed them under his foot
So we may crown him with richer hands
Than those we have today." Listen, I believe
He cares for us; I believe he sent her the nightmare
For our sake, for you and me, my sister, as a helping hand.
He is a true friend, though he sleeps below, in Hades;
No one is closer, or more dear to us both, than Father.

CHORUS:
Reverence agrees with the girl.
If your mind is sound, you'll do what she said.

444: "Dishonored, like a worthless enemy"—A killer outside of war normally would have to pay a blood price to the victim's relatives, but Clytemnestra killed Agamemnon as if he were an enemy in war and therefore did not expect to have to pay for it.

445: "Hacked off his legs"—so that his ghost would not be able to move, and so could not endanger her. This explanation comes from an ancient scholar ("a scholiast") commenting on the text. Compare Aeschylus' *Libation Bearers* 439.

445–46: "Wiped the blood . . . onto his hair"—a sign that the blood is on Agamemnon's own head, that he made himself responsible for his own death by killing Iphigenia (so an ancient commentator).

451: "Dull as it is"—a translation of the manuscript reading, which implies that her hair is dull, probably because she could not afford to dress it with fine oils or unguents. Most modern editors prefer to read a word meaning "shining" or "oily" and, by implication, "denoting supplication" (Lloyd-Jones 1994).

CHRYSÓTHEMIS:

I'll do it. Justice forbids debating on both sides
When what it demands is immediate action.
But please, for my sake, my friends,
Be quiet about it while I carry out this plan.
If Mother learns about it, bitter pain
Will strike me if I dare to carry on.

(Exit Chrysóthemis through the stage right wing.)

First Stasimon

CHORUS:

[Strophe]

Unless I have totally lost my mind
Like some raving fortune-teller,
It was Justice that spoke through that dream,
And the force of her hand will bring justice here
Very, very soon.
My confidence soared
As soon as I heard
The sweet breath of this dream.
Now there will be no forgetting:
Your father, king of the Greeks, remembers,
And so does the old bronze-made double blade
That hacked him down,
A shameful, shameful crime.

[Antistrophe]

The Fury will be here in bronze,
With a multitude of feet,

466: "Justice forbids"—perhaps stronger than the Greek. The unusual construction could mean either (1) it makes no sense to have a two-sided debate about justice, or (2) when justice clearly requires one action, no matter what, there can be no just grounds for a two-sided debate.

484: "King of the Greeks"—Agamemnon. Although he was not king of all Greeks, he was the king whom the other kings had sworn to follow in the event of war with Troy.

488: "The Fury"—Erinys, one of the divine beings that wreak vengeance on criminals who have not been punished by their victims' kin. In the *Oresteia,*

An army of hands.
She lies in ambush, terrible,
The Fury who came against
This marriage that is no marriage,
Blood drenched, forbidden.
We can be sure of this:
When people commit such crimes
Or conspire to do them with someone else,
The only miracle they can expect
Is monstrous—their own punishment.
Surely human prophecy
Cannot depend on oracles
Or on dreams of terror
Unless this vision of the night,
As we hope, comes true.

[Epode]

O Pelops! Your victory
In that old chariot race!
How painfully it weighs, endlessly,
On our land.
From the time when Myrtilus
Went to sleep beneath the sea,
Where he was tossed from a chariot of gold,
Hurled like an uprooted tree,
In a miserable crime.
After that,

Aeschylus' trilogy on this myth, as Sophocles' audience well knew, the Furies pursue Orestes after he kills his mother.

505: The chariot race of Pelops was the source of the curse on the family of Pelops, from whom Agamemnon and Aegisthus are both descended (see House of Pelops Family Tree). King Oenomaus had offered the hand of his daughter Hippodamia to the man who could beat him in a chariot race. Pelops raced Oenomaus after taking the precaution of bribing Oenomaus' charioteer—Myrtilus—to remove the linchpin on Oenomaus' vehicle (that pin keeps the wheel from sliding off the axle). Oenomaus died in the race, so Pelops was the winner. But Myrtilus claimed Hippodamia, and Pelops then threw the charioteer into the ocean. Just before Myrtilus drowned, he placed a curse on Pelops and Pelops' descendants.

This house has never been free
From the pain that flows from a crime.

(Enter Clytemnestra through the great doors. She confronts Electra.)

CLYTEMNESTRA:
So! I suppose you think you're free to roam about
Now that Aegisthus is away. He'd keep you in bounds,
Indoors, so you wouldn't be such a disgusting embarrassment
To your dear family. Well, he's gone, and you never listen
To me. And yet you have lots and lots of things to say
About me to the people. You call me cruel!
You say I rule with no regard for justice, that I treat you
Arrogantly, outrageously! But the outrage isn't coming from me.
I am only giving you back the insults you give me.
Your father—that's your only charge against me—
That his death came from me. From me!
I know that well enough. I can't deny it.
But it was justice that took him; I didn't do it alone.
And you should have helped, too, if you'd had any sense,
Because this father of yours—the one you're always
Weeping about—was the only Greek hard-hearted enough
To sacrifice a girl to the gods—your sister. The pains he took
To father her were nothing like the pain I had in giving birth.
All right. Can you convince me he had a reason to sacrifice her?
For what? For the Greeks? They had no business killing a girl
Who belonged to me. Was it for his brother Menelaus
That he killed her? If so, don't I still have a right to justice?
Didn't Menelaus have two children?
And didn't they have a better reason to die?
After all, it was their father and mother who launched those ships.
Do you think Hades had a greater appetite for my children
Than for hers? Or did your wretched father
Let his love for my children fade away
While his love was still strong for those of Menelaus?

536: "His brother Menelaus"—The Greek armada had formed to sail across to Troy and recover the beautiful Helen, who had been Menelaus' wife before she was carried off to Troy by Paris. Agamemnon and other Greek leaders had sworn to defend the marriage of Menelaus and Helen.

Would any father do these things
Unless he had foul judgment and a wicked mind?
I don't think so, though I know your mind is different.
She would agree with me, the dead girl would, if she had a voice.
As for me, I have no regrets about what I did.
Do you think I'm not making any sense? Wait till your mind
Sides with justice before you start blaming your neighbors.

ELECTRA:
This time you won't say that it was I who began
A round of insults. Still, if you permit,
I'd like to set the record straight
About my dead father and also about my sister.

CLYTEMNESTRA:
By all means, plunge ahead. If you always began
A speech this way, you wouldn't be so painful to hear.

ELECTRA:
All right, I will speak out: You admit you killed Father.
Could anything be more disgusting than that?
No! Even if you had justice on your side!
But I tell you, there was no justice in your killing.
You were controlled—brainwashed—by that wicked man,
The one you sleep with now. Would you demand an account
From Artemis, the dog driver, why she locked up the winds at Aulis?
Punishing what? I'll explain, since asking her is out of bounds.
One day, I'm told, my father went for sport
Through woods belonging to the goddess,
And there he startled a deer, a spotted buck
With antlers. He killed it, and, in doing that,

563–64: "Would you demand an account from Artemis"—Electra implies that when Clytemnestra condemns her father for sacrificing Iphigenia (530–46), she is calling Artemis to account. But the story does not do Agamemnon credit.

564: "Dog driver"—Artemis is called the "dog driver" because she is the goddess of the hunt.

565: "Asking her is out of bounds"—It would be wrong for a human being to insist that a goddess explain her actions.

He struck the goddess with an arrogant boast.
This so enraged her that she held the Greek army back,
So that my father would have to pay for his kill
By sacrificing his own daughter. That's how it was—
Her sacrificial death. The army had no other way
To move—no going home, no going on to Troy.
This forced him to do it, though he fought it hard,
And it was hard for him to sacrifice the girl. It was not
A favor to Menelaus. But suppose it was, as you claim,
And he did this to benefit his brother.
Should he die for that? At *your* hand? By whose law?
Think what you lay on yourself by imposing this law
On others. Watch out, it may be grief and repentance.
Because if we start taking a life for a life, each time
You'll be the first to die—*if* justice comes your way.
Take care: Your plea of justice will not stand.
Please, if you like, convince me you had cause
To commit your own more recent foul, disgusting crimes:
One, you are sleeping with a man whose hands
Are stained with blood (your helper, back then, in killing
  Father);
Two, you are making babies while you turn the ones you had
Back then into outcasts, although they had grown up true
To the family and from a true marriage. For these two crimes
How can I say a single word of praise? Are you telling me
That you did them to avenge your daughter?
Ridiculous! Whatever you say, it's disgusting
To marry an enemy to get even for a daughter's death.
Yet I am not allowed to say a single word against you
Without you shouting to the whole wide world
That I have a filthy mouth. And what are you to me?
More tyrant than mother, in my judgment.
My life is a misery; I bed down with pain
And endless anguish all because of you—and him,
Your partner. As for the one of us who got away,

570: "Arrogant boast"—Agamemnon killed a sacred deer in a sacred precinct and claimed credit for it, thus insulting Artemis.

589: "You are making babies"—Among the children of Aegisthus and Clytemnestra was a daughter, Erigone. According to one story, she was the mother of Orestes' illegitimate son, Penthilus.

Orestes, he suffers still, though you can't reach him now.
You keep accusing me of raising him to wash away
Blood-guilt by vengeance. Well, if I had the strength,
I would have done it for sure. Because of him, you blare
Insults at me from the rooftops: "Wicked slut" you say,
Or "foul-mouthed," or "no sense of shame at all."
All right, if I was born like that, it came from you.
So I have my mother's nature: I'm not ashamed of that.

CHORUS:
I see she is huffing with anger. Is she giving any thought
To whether justice is on her side? I don't see that yet.

CLYTEMNESTRA:
What kind of thought should I have toward her?
She treats her mother so outrageously—and at her age, too!
Don't you understand? She has no sense of shame.
She'd stop at nothing, no matter how disgusting.

ELECTRA:
Listen, of course I am ashamed of what I do,
Even if you can't tell. I learn from what I see,
And so I act in ways that are not right for me.
It's all because you hate me so much.
You absolutely force me to act the way I do.
You know: "Act ugly, ugly actions teach."

610: "I see she is huffing with anger"—Who is the chorus referring to—Electra or Clytemnestra? The text is unclear. Perhaps the chorus leader is referring to Electra and telling Clytemnestra that Electra's anger has drowned her attempt at rational argument. That is Jebb's (1894) view, supported by his comparison with Sophocles' *Antigone* 471. Other scholars think the anger is Clytemnestra's and indicated by the actor's gesture. In that case, the chorus leader would be talking to Electra and referring to Clytemnestra, whose appearance, behind the mask, would need to be made explicit by a speaker. On the one hand, the chorus in such a context usually comments on the preceding speech; on the other, Clytemnestra takes the comment of the chorus as directed toward her, as we see from the following line. So either interpretation may be defended.

621: "Act ugly, ugly actions teach"—apparently, a proverb. The word translated "ugly"—the opposite of "beautiful," "noble"—is often translated as "shameful" or "disgusting."

CLYTEMNESTRA:
You nasty bitch! So I'm to blame! Really?
My words, my actions—they're making you talk too much?

ELECTRA:
It's you. You're the one who's talking, not me.
The action was yours, and action is the cause of words.

CLYTEMNESTRA:
My god! By Artemis, I swear you'll pay for this
Insolence. Just wait till Aegisthus is home.

ELECTRA:
Look at that! You just flew into a rage! You said I could say
What I want, but you don't know how to listen!

CLYTEMNESTRA:
Won't you let me make my sacrifice? A decent silence, please;
No more shouting. I let you say everything you wanted.

ELECTRA:
Make your sacrifice! My lips are sealed.
I won't say another word that offends you.

CLYTEMNESTRA:

(To a servant, who is carrying a tray of garden-grown offerings.)

Then I ask you to stand by me and lift up
These bountiful offerings so that I may raise a prayer
To this lord to release me from the fears that I have now.

(To the statue.)

Hear my words I pray, Apollo, guardian of our house,
And understand their secret meaning. I am not among friends,
And it would be a mistake for me to bring everything
Openly into the light while she is standing next to me.
If I did, her tongue is so busy screaming in anger
That she'd spread false, malicious words all over the city.
So listen to me as I asked, since this is how I'll speak.

638: "I am not among friends"—Clytemnestra is trying to convey her meaning about the dream to Apollo while concealing it from Electra, her enemy. She does not know that Electra has already heard the content of the dream.

The images I saw last night in that dream with two meanings—
O Wolf-slayer, if what they promise is good,
Grant that they may come true! But if not,
If what they promise is hostile, send them back
Against my enemies. And if anyone has a secret plot
To throw me out of my position of wealth, don't let them.
But allow me to live my life, as before, in total safety,
Looking after this house and the royal power
Of the sons of Atreus. Allow me to share
Day after day of happiness with my friends
And my children—the ones who do not hate me
Or carry bitter pain. For these things, Apollo
Wolf-slayer, I pray. Hear me graciously,
And grant us all that we request. What I've not said
I believe you understand, though I am silent.
As a god, as a son of Zeus, you must know everything.

(Enter the Tutor through the stage right wing.)

TUTOR:
Greetings to you, women. As your guest, I ask if I can be
Certain that this is the house of the tyrant Aegisthus.

CHORUS:
It is here, my friend. Your guess was right.

TUTOR:
Now I am also guessing that this is the woman in charge.
Am I right? She looks like a ruler.

644: "That dream with two meanings"—literally, "that double dream," the one described at 417–23. The meaning depends on which king is represented by the branching scepter. If it is Aegisthus, the dream is good for Clytemnestra because it means their son will rule. But if it is Agamemnon, as she fears, then it means that Orestes will recover the kingdom.

645: "Wolf-slayer"—literally, "Wolfish." This phrase could also be translated "Lord of Light," but here Clytemnestra is most likely thinking of Apollo as the god who protects the family from threats such as wolves. See note on 6.

652: "The sons of Atreus"—Agamemnon and Menelaus.

661: "Tyrant"—a word that need not carry an offensive meaning. The irony here is that it does carry a negative connotation to the Tutor (as it would to the Athenian audience), but not to Clytemnestra.

CHORUS:
She certainly is. And she's right there beside you.

TUTOR:
I wish you joy, lady. I am here with a report from a friend.
It will be a pleasure for you to hear and for Aegisthus as well.

CLYTEMNESTRA:
What a good omen! I accept it. But first,
I must know who it was that sent you to me.

TUTOR:
Phanoteus of Phocis. And the matter is weighty.

CLYTEMNESTRA:
What is it, visitor? Tell me. It comes from a man
Who is our friend, as I know clearly, so I expect friendly news.

TUTOR:
Orestes is dead, to put it succinctly.

ELECTRA:
Oh no! Misery! I'm finished. Today's the end for me.

CLYTEMNESTRA:
What are you saying? What are you saying? Don't listen to her.

TUTOR:
Orestes is dead. I said it once; I'll say it again.

ELECTRA:
I'm finished. A miserable nothing. It's all over for me now.

CLYTEMNESTRA: *(To Electra.)*
Mind your own business and get to work. Now you,
Visitor. Tell me the truth: In what way did he die?

TUTOR:
I was sent on this mission, so I will tell you everything.
Orestes came to the glorious showplace of Greece
To compete for prizes in the Delphic Games.

670: "Phanoteus of Phocis"—a special friend of Aegisthus and Clytemnestra; Phocis is the place where Orestes grew safely to manhood. See note on 45 and map.

682: Delphic Games—See note on 49. During the Pythian Festival at Delphi there were contests in the arts, in athletics, and in racing chariots and

And when he had heard the announcer, in a great voice,
Call for the footrace, the very first event,
He entered it. His body had a glow
That struck awe into everyone. He completed the course
As well as he began it and came out with the prize.
Well, to make a long story short for you,
I never knew such a man for winning prizes.
This much is certain: In every race the referee announced,
The one on the double track and all the usual ones,
He carried off the wreaths of victory.
Everyone thought he was blessed with happiness,
And they hailed him as Orestes from Argos, the son
Of Agamemnon, who, once upon a time,
Mustered the glorious army of Greece. And so it was.
But when a god is being destructive, there is no strength
That can escape. So, on another day,
When the chariot race was set to begin at dawn,
He entered the swift contest against many charioteers.
One was Achaean, one from Sparta, and two
Of them were expert yoke-masters from Libya.
There was one who had horses from Thessaly
(He was the fifth); the sixth came from Aetolia
And was driving chestnut fillies. The seventh was
Magnesian; the eighth, with white horses, was Aenian;
The ninth one came from Athens, a city built by gods.
And there was a Boeotian, who manned the tenth chariot.
They took their places where the appointed referees,
After casting lots, assigned each vehicle.
Then, at a trumpet blast, they were off like a shot,
Cheering on their horses with one voice, snapping the reins.
Then all the racecourse was bursting with sound,
The clatter and clash of chariots, and the dust
Billowed up. Soon they were all in a close pack,

---

horses, in that order. The chariot race took the form of laps between turning posts. For Homer's account of such a race, see Book 23 of the *Iliad*.

686–87: "He completed the course / As well as he began it."—The translation follows an emendation, as interpreted by Kells (1973). The manuscripts read: "He made the endpoints of the course equal to his nature," which might mean, "He ran as well as he looked."

Goading their horses like mad, each one trying
To pass the other's axle and snorting horses,
For everywhere their flanks and their spinning wheels
Were spattered with foam from horses' panting breath.
Now, at each turn, Orestes kept close to the post,
Just touching it with his axle-housing and giving
His right-hand horse free rein to block the next team.
At first, they all stayed upright in their chariots,
But then the Aenian racer lost control
Of his colts—they were too hard mouthed to feel
The bridle—right at the turn at the end of the sixth lap.
As the seventh lap began, his colts dashed their heads
On a chariot from Libya. Then one piled into another
In a single disaster of broken, colliding chariots, and the whole
Plain of Crisa was filled with the wreckage of horse-gear.
Seeing this, the Athenian, who was an expert with reins,
Jerked his team aside and held them back
So he avoided the maelstrom of horses at the center.
Orestes was driving in the first lane, holding his colts
Just behind the others, trusting in a strong finish.
When he saw that only one other remained on the course,
He barked a sharp command into his horses' ears
And gave chase. The two were driving yoke to yoke;
Now one, now the other, took the lead,
But never by more than a horse's head.
Now, during all the laps so far, Orestes drove safely,
And the poor man kept his vehicle straight and upright.
But then he slacked off on the left-hand reins
As the horse was turning—he wasn't paying attention.
He crashed against the post, shattered
His axle-housing, dived over the railing,
Got tangled in the cut-leather reins. As he fell,
His horses skittered off into the middle of the course.
The people, when they saw he was thrown from his chariot,
Were wailing with pity for this young man,
Who, after doing such great deeds, had wound up
In such a disaster. Now he was thrown in the dust,
Now tossed to the sky, his legs flashing, until drivers,
With great difficulty, got his horses under control.
Then they cut him free, but he was such a wreck
Of blood and gore that his friends would not know him.

They burned him right away, and now a little bronze
Holds that magnificent body's miserable ashes.
Men of Phocis were chosen to bring him here
So that he could be buried in the land of his father.
So it came about. It is painful enough to hear
A report, but to see it, as we did,
Why, it was the worst disaster I have ever seen.

CHORUS: *(With groans of horror.)*
The ruling family
Is wiped out like an uprooted tree.

CLYTEMNESTRA:
O Zeus! What can I say? Is it good luck?
Or horrible? But is it to my advantage?
What agony this is—I save my life by losing so much!

TUTOR:
Why are you so downhearted, lady, at this news?

CLYTEMNESTRA:
It's wonderful and horrible to be a mother—
Even when he treats you badly, you cannot hate your child.

TUTOR:
Apparently we should not have come. It was a waste of time.

CLYTEMNESTRA:
No, not at all, no waste of time. How could it be?
Not if you have brought with you compelling evidence
That he is dead. He was born out of my life,
But he tore himself from my breasts and the care I gave him,
Ran away, and became a foreigner. And since the time
He left us he has never seen me. But he blames me
For his father's death, and he makes terrible threats.
And so for all these nights and days I have never had
The sweet shelter of sleep. But every passing moment
Has come over me as the moment of my death.

And now, today, I have been set free. I have no more fear
Of him. Or of this woman here. *(Pointing to Electra.)*
She's done me more harm.
She lives with me, you see, and she sucks my lifeblood
Constantly. But from now on, peace and calm
Will guard our days from all her threats.

ELECTRA:
No! It's too horrible! Orestes, must I grieve for you?
Now, while your mother abuses you arrogantly
In your downfall? Could this be good?

CLYTEMNESTRA:
Not for you. But things, as they stand, stand well for him.

ELECTRA:
Nemesis! Are you listening? Come, protect the dead.

CLYTEMNESTRA:
Nemesis heard what she should have heard; her ruling was good.

ELECTRA:
Go ahead—abuse me. Now that luck is on your side.

CLYTEMNESTRA:
Won't you put a stop to this, you and Orestes?

ELECTRA:
We have been stopped, and now we can't stop you.

CLYTEMNESTRA: *(To the Tutor.)*
Your visit, sir, deserves a great reward
If you have stopped her screaming voice.

TUTOR:
Then I should be off now that all is well.

CLYTEMNESTRA:
Certainly not. You deserve better,
And so does the friend who sent you.
Come right in; leave this woman outside.
Let her bawl over her troubles out here.

(Exit the Tutor, ushered by Clytemnestra, through the great doors.)

790: "Could this be good?"—Lloyd-Jones (1994) follows an emendation that means, "Am I not well off?"

791: "Not for you . . . stand well for him"—Orestes, at least, is past doing any harm to Clytemnestra.

792: Nemesis—goddess of righteous vengeance.

ELECTRA: *(To the chorus.)*
Do *you* think she had pain behind those groans?
And was it horror—or cleverness—that made her weep
And wail? A sad woman mourning for her son?
I jeered at her, but I myself have passed away. Orestes!
Orestes! Your death wipes me out.
When you went away, you ripped hope out of my mind,
The only hope left to me—for you to be alive
And come avenge your father. And me.
Now where can I turn? I am alone,
Bereft. You and Father both are gone.
For a long time now I've been a slave
To people I detest, my worst enemies,
My father's killers. Could this be right?
No! I'll never go back inside.
I'll never be at home again. I'll stay here
At the gate, now that I have no friend or family,
And let my life fade away. Or let *them* kill me—
The people inside—if I bother them. It'd be a favor
To be killed! Life is pain. I do not want to live.

[Strophe *a*]

CHORUS:
Where is Zeus' thunderbolt now? Where is shining Apollo?
How can they watch this scene from their hiding places?
Why don't they do something?

ELECTRA: *(A loud cry.)*
Aaah! Aaah!

CHORUS:
Dear child! Why so loud?

ELECTRA: *(Louder.)*
Aaah! Horrible!

CHORUS:
Don't make so much noise when you cry!

822–70: This passage in lyric meter, with the balanced structure of a choral ode, expresses Electra's powerful emotions and is known as a *kommos*.

ELECTRA:
You're killing me!

CHORUS:
How?

ELECTRA:
If you are going to pretend there's hope
When anyone can see they've gone to Hades,
You'll just be trampling a woman who is already down.

[Antistrophe *a*]

CHORUS:
But I know about Amphiaraus, the lord of seers.
After he had been caught by a woman
In a golden necklace and hidden away
Beneath the earth . . .

ELECTRA: *(A loud cry.)*
Aaah! Aaah!

CHORUS:
Still, he rules; his soul is intact.

ELECTRA: *(Louder.)*
Aaah! Horrible!

CHORUS:
Yes, indeed. Horrible. The guilty woman . . .

ELECTRA:
Was curbed.

CHORUS:
Yes.

834: Hades—the Underworld.

836: Amphiaraus—Amphiaraus' wife Eriphyle was bribed with a golden necklace to persuade him to go to war, so he joined the army of Argos that was led by Oedipus' son Polynices, who hoped to recover the throne of Thebes. After the army's momentous defeat at the seven gates, Amphiaraus was swallowed by the earth and honored as a semidivine prophetic hero. Eriphyle—who had been bribed a second time—persuaded Alcmaeon, Amphiaraus' son, to join in a second attempt on Thebes. On Alcmaeon's return, he punished Eriphyle with death.

ELECTRA:
I know, I know.
That unhappy man had an avenger come to light.
But for me—no one. The one I had has gone away,
Stolen from me.

[Strophe *b*]

CHORUS:
Misery meets misery in you.

ELECTRA:
On misery I am an expert, more than an expert:
My life has been tossed in every flood of horror,
Every month of every year.

CHORUS:
We understand why you lament.

ELECTRA:
No, not anymore. Don't
Try to divert me when there's no . . .

CHORUS:
No what?

ELECTRA:
No hope left to us; no one new will be born
From our ancient family to defend us.

[Antistrophe *b*]

CHORUS:
All mortals are born to die.

ELECTRA:
But are they born for a chariot wreck?
To crash, like him? To be caught
In a whip of harness, a flash of hooves?

CHORUS:
It's a horror beyond imagining.

864: "Beyond imagining"—The Greek here ranges in meaning from "unlooked for" to "incredible" and from that to "unconscionable," as Lloyd-Jones (1994) renders it.

ELECTRA:
How could anyone have imagined it?
He died in a strange land
Where I could not lay him out with my own hands.

(The chorus emit a sympathetic cry.)

ELECTRA:
He was simply put underground
Without a funeral,
And I was not there to weep for him.

(Enter Chrysóthemis, excited and in haste, through the stage right wing.)

CHRYSÓTHEMIS:
I am so excited by joy, dear sister, that I came
Back in a rush. It's no time for decorum;
I bring news of joy. This is the end
Of all those troubles you've been weeping about.

ELECTRA:
You? Where would *you* find an antidote?
The pain is mine; it is beyond cure.

CHRYSÓTHEMIS:
He's here with us! Orestes! Listen to me:
He's here, as sure as you're seeing me now.

ELECTRA:
Have you lost your mind? You're in a sorry state—
This is your disaster, too. It's not a joke.

CHRYSÓTHEMIS:
No, by Father's hearthstone! It's no joke;
I'm not abusing you. He's right nearby.

ELECTRA:
You *are* in a sad way. Who in the whole wide world
Could make you believe a tale like that so strongly?

CHRYSÓTHEMIS:
Me, myself. No one else. I saw the evidence,
Clear enough to prove that the story is true.

ELECTRA:
What was the evidence you saw, poor thing?
It warmed you with all the comfort . . . of a deadly fire!

CHRYSÓTHEMIS:
For gods' sake, listen to me tell the whole story.
Then you'll know if I am a sensible woman or a fool.

ELECTRA:
Tell the story, then, if talking makes you happy.

CHRYSÓTHEMIS:
All right, I'll tell you exactly everything I saw.
When I came to Father's tomb on the ancient mound,
I saw fresh streams of milk springing from the top,
And all the flowers that are in bloom
Were twisted in a wreath to crown Father's grave.
I saw this and I was amazed. I looked around,
Thinking someone else might be there with me.
But stillness was all I could find in that place,
So I crept up on the tomb, and at the edge I saw,
On the burial site, a freshly cut lock of hair.
Then immediately my poor soul was struck
With a long-familiar precious sight—the man I love
More than anyone, Orestes. This was evidence of him!
I took and felt it with my hands, not daring to say a word,
But joy immediately filled my eyes with tears.
And now I know for sure, as I did then:
This lovely gift could only have come from him.
Who else is supposed to do this? Only me and you.
Me, I did not do it—that's for sure.
And neither did you, because if you leave this house
Even to visit a shrine, you're made to regret it.
And as for Mother, her mind does not incline that way,
And if she'd done a thing like that, we'd have seen her.

894–96: Chrysóthemis is describing an ordinary offering at a tomb, but her imagery—rivulets and springs of milk, flowers of every kind—suggests a miracle.

903: "A long-familiar precious sight"—a mental image of Orestes as he must be, now that he has grown up. It is familiar because she has imagined it so often, during her long wait for his arrival.

So Orestes is the one who left these burial gifts.
So cheer up, dear sister; the same people
Do not always have the same run of luck.
Ours has been dreadful up to now. But today,
Perhaps, will guarantee us a brilliant future.

ELECTRA:
You don't have a clue. As you talked, I pitied you.

CHRYSÓTHEMIS:
What? Aren't you happy about my news?

ELECTRA:
You don't know what path or plan you are following.

CHRYSÓTHEMIS:
What do you mean? I saw it with my own eyes!

ELECTRA:
He's dead. I am sorry. All hope of him is gone.
He won't save us. Don't expect anything from him.

CHRYSÓTHEMIS:
Don't say that! Who told you this?

ELECTRA:
A man who was beside him when he died.

CHRYSÓTHEMIS:
So where is he now? I'm amazed; I'm overcome.

ELECTRA:
In the house, where Mother is delighted with him, not pained.

CHRYSÓTHEMIS:
No, don't say this. Then who could it possibly be
Who made all those offerings at Father's tomb?

ELECTRA:
My best guess is they're for Orestes now that he's dead,
Put there as a memorial by someone or other.

CHRYSÓTHEMIS:
This is terrible! I came in such a hurry to bring
You this joyful news, but I did not really know
How deeply we were ruined. Now that I'm here—
Our old reality was horrible, but I find this far worse.

ELECTRA:
That's how things are with you, but listen to me:
You can shake off the weight of all this grief.

CHRYSÓTHEMIS:
What am I going to do—raise the dead?

ELECTRA:
That was not my point. I wasn't born a fool.

CHRYSÓTHEMIS:
So what are you asking me to do that I can do?

ELECTRA:
To have the courage to do as I direct.

CHRYSÓTHEMIS:
If it will help us, I won't refuse.

ELECTRA:
But look, it will be tough. No pain, no happiness.

CHRYSÓTHEMIS:
I see. I'll take as tough a load as I can bear.

ELECTRA:
Pay attention now; here's my plan:
You know as well as I we've no friends here to help;
There's no one left for us. Hades took them all
And left us solitary and bereft. Now, as for me,
So long as I was told our brother lived
And flourished, I had hopes that someday soon
He'd take on the job and avenge our father's death.
But now that he's no more, it's you I'm looking at.
This red-handed murderer who killed Father—
You won't hesitate, will you?—kill Aegisthus!
I don't need to hide things from you any longer.
Look! How could you go on living otherwise?
What can you hope for to set things right? When a girl
Inherits from her father nothing but grief—
None of his wealth—then what is her legacy,
Aside from time to grow old? She ages her life away,
Unmarried and unwedded. Hopeless.
Would Aegisthus ever allow either you or me

To carry on our family and breed a new generation
Of threats to him? It's obvious: No one could be so stupid.
But if you adopt my plan, here's what will happen:
First, you'll earn sacred goodwill from both
Of those who are dead and buried, our father and our brother.
On top of that, you'll call yourself what you were born to be—
A free woman—and after that you'll win
A husband of your social rank. All men
Are dazzled by success. You'll never have
So much fame unless you throw in with me.
And anyone who sees you then, citizen or foreigner—
Wouldn't he heap you with praise? Wouldn't he say,
"Look, my friends, this is the pair of sisters
Who saved their father's house. They staked their lives
On this, when their enemies were well ensconced,
To bring them to account for murder.
Everyone should love and treat them with respect.
In festivals or assemblies of the city, everyone
Should honor them for manly courage." That
Is the way they all will boast about us then,
And glorious fame will follow us in life or death
Forever. So trust me, sister dear; do as I say.
Take up the burden of our father's pain!
Take up our brother's trouble! Release me
From evil! Release yourself! And keep this in mind:
It's shameful for well-born folk to live in disgrace.

CHORUS:
In a case like this, you should think ahead.
Forethought is your ally, whether you speak or listen.

CHRYSÓTHEMIS:

(To the chorus.)

Yes, my friends. And if she were endowed with an intellect
That was not so badly flawed, she would have taken care
To be discreet, which she certainly has not been.

(To Electra.)

What could you possibly expect from this? You lift
Your fierceness like a sword, and you ask me for support?

Can't you see? You're a woman—that's your nature.
You're not a man; you're not as strong as your enemies in a fight.
Good luck is blooming for them, growing by the day.
For us, it is draining away; it goes to nothing.
Could anyone hope to take down a man like that
And come away without agony, without ruin?
Our troubles are bad enough, so you'd best take care:
They'd be worse if someone heard what you just said.
It won't save us and it won't do us any good
To become famous on our way to a disgraceful death.
I don't hate dying so much as not having the power
To die when that would be a blessing.
So I beg of you, before we are totally destroyed,
Before our family is wiped clean away,
Contain your anger! Now, all those things you've said—
I'll not let them be said again. They're null and void.
Please be sensible for once in this long time,
And, since you are so weak, give in to our rulers.

CHORUS:
Do as she says. Foresight always gives the best
Advantage to human beings. That, and wisdom.

ELECTRA:
Just as I expected! I knew perfectly well
You'd toss my proposal away.
So. I'm single-handed: I'll have to do this thing
Alone. I'll never let it go.

CHRYSÓTHEMIS:
Oh,
How I wish you'd had a plan like that when Father died.
You could have overcome everything.

ELECTRA:
I was as strong by nature then, but not so strong-minded.

1007–8: Some editors consider these lines an interpolation.

1023–27: These lines play on the Greek word for "mind," *nous,* which here ranges in meaning from "mind" to "good intention" and "good sense."

CHRYSÓTHEMIS:
You should train your mind always to be the same.

ELECTRA:
So you won't help me take action—you want me to mind you?

CHRYSÓTHEMIS:
Because if you start this way, I expect you'll end badly.

ELECTRA:
I do admire your mind; it's your cowardice I hate.

CHRYSÓTHEMIS:
I'll accept what you say, too, when I hear compliments.

ELECTRA:
You'll never hear compliments from me.

CHRYSÓTHEMIS:
Time will tell, and there's plenty of it left.

ELECTRA:
Get out of here! You're no use at all.

CHRYSÓTHEMIS:
I am, too. But you don't know anything.

ELECTRA:
You'll run to your mother and tell her everything.

CHRYSÓTHEMIS:
I don't hate you that much. Really, I don't.

ELECTRA:
But don't you see you're leading me into disgrace?

CHRYSÓTHEMIS:
Disgrace, no. Thinking ahead, yes. For your own sake.

ELECTRA:
Do I really have to obey your rules of justice?

CHRYSÓTHEMIS:
Come to your senses, and you'll be leading us both.

ELECTRA:
It's horrible to speak so well and be so wrong!

CHRYSÓTHEMIS:
You're quite right—speaking of yourself.

ELECTRA:
What? You can't think that you're speaking on the side of justice.

CHRYSÓTHEMIS:
No. There's a time when even justice causes harm.

ELECTRA:
I should live by those laws? They're not for me.

CHRYSÓTHEMIS:
Do what you want. You'll respect me afterward.

ELECTRA:
Of course I'll do what I want. You don't scare me.

CHRYSÓTHEMIS:
Is this really true? You won't discuss it and reconsider?

ELECTRA:
Discuss it? What could be more hateful than discussion with a coward?

CHRYSÓTHEMIS:
I don't think you have any idea what I am talking about.

ELECTRA:
It was ages ago that I made this decision, not just recently.

CHRYSÓTHEMIS:
Then I'll leave. My words will never earn your respect,
And, the way you're going, your actions will never earn mine.

ELECTRA:
OK, go inside then. I'll never follow you,
No matter how passionately you want me to do so.
It's pure foolishness, chasing phantoms.

CHRYSÓTHEMIS:
OK. So you claim these decisions of yours

1050–54: Lloyd-Jones and Wilson (1990a) considers these lines an interpolation. The word *epainein* translated as "respect" normally means "praise."

Are good thinking. Then go ahead and think that way.
Later, when you're in bad trouble, you'll respect what I said.

(Exit Chrysóthemis through the great doors.)

Second Stasimon

CHORUS:

[Strophe *a*]

Birds above are wisest.
We watch them tend the needs
Of those from whom they grew
And those who were good to them.
Why don't we do the same?
But the time will come—
The thunderbolt of Zeus,
The dictate of heaven will bring it on—
Soon people will pay, in anguish.

O voice that cries to the dead in the earth,
Shriek into the ears of Agamemnon down below
For my sake and tell him, "Shame!"

[Antistrophe *a*]

Tell him his home is now tormented
With plague. His children
Shout battle cries at one another;
Family love is drowned.
The girl who weeps alone
Endlessly for her father's death,
This girl has been abandoned to the storms;
She cries in misery
Like a plaintive nightingale.

She would give her life and leave the light
If only she could bring the Furies down on both!

1058: "Birds above are wisest"—Storks proverbially looked after their parents. The contrast is evidently being made to Agamemnon's children, who still, after so many years, have not avenged his killing.

Has any other hero's daughter burst into such bloom?

[Strophe *b*]

No one from a fine family
Who is forced to live like garbage
Would ever trade her glory
For the shame of silence.
Oh, child, dear child, what a public spectacle
You have made of your misery!
You put on the full armor against shame,
So now your name is two in one:
You are "the wise-and-good."

[Antistrophe *b*]

I pray you will rise as high
On the palm of wealth as now you sink
Beneath the hand of your enemies.
Although I see you now
Caught in a horrible life,
The laws that grew strongest
Will give you victory
Because of your reverence for Zeus.

(Enter Orestes and Pylades through the stage right wing. Pylades is carrying a small brass burial urn.)

ORESTES:
Greetings! Did we hear right? Are we
On the right road for where we need to be?

CHORUS:
What are you looking for? What brought you here?

1081: "Has any . . . such bloom?"—Deliberately ambiguous, this succinct line refers at once to Electra's noble birth, her self-sacrificing loyalty to her father, and the horror of her present circumstances.

1095: "The laws that grew strongest"—The verb "grew" suggests a natural growth, as in plants. Accordingly, most scholars have identified these laws with those of nature, such as the laws followed by the storks and by Electra, but not by her siblings. The chorus represents these siblings as unnatural human beings (see 1058 ff.).

ORESTES:
Aegisthus—I've been asking where he lives.

CHORUS:
You've come right. Your guide was faultless.

ORESTES:
Is there one of you who could tell the family
About our group's arrival? It has been eagerly awaited.

CHORUS: *(Pointing to Electra.)*
She could, if you want to ask the closest relative.

ORESTES:
Miss, could you go inside and tell them
That some men from Phocis are asking for Aegisthus?

ELECTRA:
Oh no! Don't tell me that what you're carrying is proof—
Visible proof—of the story we have heard.

ORESTES:
I don't know what rumor you heard, but an old man
Named Strophius sent us with news about Orestes.

ELECTRA:
What is it? How quickly fear comes over me!

ORESTES:
Here is the little that remains of him. He's dead.
As you can see, the urn we bring is very small.

ELECTRA:
Oh, misery! So this is it. It's clear.
So now I see this heavy load straight on.

ORESTES:
Are you weeping over Orestes' sad fate?
Then you should know: This is the container for his body.

ELECTRA:
Visitor, give it to me, please, right now.
Is he really hidden in this urn? Let me hold it

1111: Strophius—the king in Phocis who had been Orestes' host while he grew up there. Strophius is an ally of Agamemnon, while his uncle and hereditary enemy, Phanoteus, is an ally of Aegisthus. See 45 and 670, with notes.

In my own hands. I need to weep and mourn
Over these ashes for me and my whole family.

ORESTES: *(To Pylades.)*
Here, give this to the woman, whoever she is.
There's no hostility in her request; she must be
Close to the family, perhaps a blood relative.

ELECTRA:
So this is all I have to remember him.
No one was closer to me than Orestes. I sent him off
With such high hopes, and I'm taking him back
With none. This thing I hold in my hands
Is nothing. But you, my child, were a blaze of light
When I sent you from home. I should have died
Before these hands stole you and sent you abroad.
I saved you from murder, but I stole from you
The opportunity to die at home, on the same day
As Father, and to be buried with him in his tomb.
But as it was, you were on foreign ground, a refugee.
What a horrible way to die—cut off from your sister!
So I could not take your body in my own
Dear hands and grieve, and bathe, and lay you out.
And I could not rake the sad burden of bones
Out of the scorching coals, as I should have done.
It was foreign hands that put your little remnant
In a little urn. Now I weep for the times gone by
When I would care for you. What a waste that was—
All the sweet trouble I took for you!
You never belonged to Mother as much as to me.
I loved you more than she did. No servants looked after you
But me. You always called me "Sister."
Now all of this has been lost in one day,
The day you died. You swept everything away
Like a tornado, and you are gone. Father's gone.
I'm dead, thanks to you. You're absolutely dead.
Laughter from our enemies! A wild rage of joy
From our mother—*un*-mother, I mean—the one you said
(By secret messages) that you would come
And punish on your own. But now our demon luck,
Yours and mine, has ripped this away from us.

All it's given us, instead of your dear shape,
Is ash and shadow.
I am so miserable.
Pity this poor corpse!

(She cries in grief.)

Frightful, horrible, the paths you had to take.
You destroyed me,
Really destroyed me, my dear brother.
So take me now under this roof of yours;
Take this nothing into nothing so that I may be at home,
Below, with you, forever after. While you were above,
I was your equal partner. Now I beg to be
With you, to die and never leave your tomb
Because I see the dead are free from pain.

CHORUS:
You come from a father who was subject to death,
Electra. Keep that in mind. Orestes too is mortal,
So do not mourn too much. We all must die.

ORESTES:
Oh no! What can I say? Words fail me.
I do not have the strength to control my tongue.

ELECTRA:
You're in pain suddenly. Why? What is this about?

ORESTES:
You look like someone famous. Are you Electra?

ELECTRA:
I am. And I am in total agony.

ORESTES: *(With a cry of grief.)*
How sadly things turned out for you!

ELECTRA:
It's not possible—you're a visitor. Why weep for me?

ORESTES:
They've made a wreck of your body—what contempt! What godlessness!

ELECTRA:
You're talking about me? Why are you so sad?

ORESTES:
What misery! Not married, not enough food.

ELECTRA:
Why are you looking at me this way, weeping?

ORESTES:
I had no idea how rotten my situation was.

ELECTRA:
How could you learn this from what you've heard?

ORESTES:
Because I see you; your suffering is so conspicuous.

ELECTRA:
But really, you're seeing only a few of my troubles.

ORESTES:
Could anything be more hateful than what I see now?

ELECTRA:
Yes, because I live and feed with the murderers.

ORESTES:
Of whom? Where'd this trouble come from? Be clear.

ELECTRA:
My father. I am the slave of the people who murdered him.

ORESTES:
Someone's compelling you to live like this: Who is it?

ELECTRA:
She's called my mother. But she's nothing like a mother.

ORESTES:
What does she do? Lay hands on you? Starve you?

ELECTRA:
Lay hands and starve and everything.

ORESTES:
Isn't there anyone to help or protect you?

1183: "Not married"— See 165 and note.

ELECTRA:
No, there was. But you gave me his ashes.

ORESTES:
It's so hard! The moment I saw you I pitied you.

ELECTRA:
The only one who's ever pitied me is you. That's for sure.

ORESTES:
The only one! Well, I am here. And your pain is mine.

ELECTRA:
You're not some relative of ours, are you, from somewhere?

ORESTES:
I'd like to tell you. Are these people on our side?

ELECTRA:
Yes, they are. You can talk safely.

ORESTES:
Then set this urn aside if you want to learn everything.

ELECTRA:
For gods' sake, stranger, don't do this to me!

ORESTES: *(Trying to relieve her of the burden of the urn.)*
Put this container down, and I'll tell you everything.

ELECTRA:
No! It's what I love most. As you are a man, don't take it!

ORESTES:
You can't keep it.

ELECTRA:
This is horrible!
Orestes, if I am not allowed to bury you . . .

ORESTES:
Careful what you say. It's wrong for you to weep.

ELECTRA:
How could it be wrong? It's my brother who died!

ORESTES:
It's not for you to say this.

ELECTRA:
Have I lost the right to mourn for him? How?

ORESTES:
You haven't lost any rights. This isn't yours.

ELECTRA:
Of course it is! If what I hold is the body of Orestes.

ORESTES:
It's not Orestes. That was just a story we made up.

ELECTRA:
Then where is the poor man's casket?

ORESTES:
There isn't one. A living man doesn't have a casket.

ELECTRA:
What did you say, my child?

ORESTES:
Nothing false.

ELECTRA:
Is the man alive?

ORESTES:
If I am breathing.

ELECTRA:
Is it you?

ORESTES: *(Showing her his signet ring.)*
Look at this seal—
It was my father's—then you'll know.

ELECTRA:
O my dearest light!

ORESTES:
Dearest, I swear.

ELECTRA:
Your voice, it's here!

ORESTES:
No need to hear from others now.

ELECTRA:
I have you in my arms!

ORESTES:
And forever after.

ELECTRA:
Dearest women, women of the city,
Look, here's Orestes. It was only a trick
That he was dead, and that trick has kept him alive!

CHORUS:
We see him, dear child. Such good luck!
Joy brings tears to our eyes.

[Strophe]

ELECTRA:
O beloved seed, beloved child,
You're here now.
You found; you came; you saw those you longed for.

ORESTES:
Yes, we're here. But keep it quiet.

ELECTRA:
Why?

ORESTES:
Quiet is better, so no one inside hears.

ELECTRA:
No, by Artemis,
Goddess undominated, always unmarried!
I will never consent to tremble

1225: "No need to hear from others now"—literally, "No longer inquire from any another source." For all these years, Electra had to hear news of Orestes from other people.

1231–87: Second Kommos—Once again, strong emotion sends the speakers into balanced stanzas of lyric meter, here broken into dialogue. The actors would sing the lines for greater emotional impact on the audience.

At the women who stay indoors,
That wasteful burden on the land.

ORESTES:
But look, there's war in women, too.
You learned that from your own experience.

ELECTRA:
O pain, pain, pain!
This evil thing you've brought up,
Not covered by clouds,
Never to be dispersed,
Never to be forgotten,
This evil, which we have by birth.

ORESTES:
I know this very well. But wait till their arrival
Prompts us; then we should remember what they did.

[Antistrophe]

ELECTRA:
Every time is the right time for me, every moment;

1242: "That wasteful burden on the land"—words that would remind the Greek audience of the Homeric idea that nobles who do not fight are a useless burden on farmland. See Homer's *Iliad* 12.310–21. Electra lays this charge on women, but that is unfair. Women traditionally did a great deal of work, especially weaving.

1246–50: "This evil thing . . . which we have by birth"—Electra and Orestes have had a painful experience of the spirit of war that is in women from their mother, and the murder of their father has left them forever spotlighted by evil. One editor reads 1247 differently—"covered by clouds" (Kells 1973)—because Greek rarely portrays evil as being bright; but this evil is, as we would say in English, glaring.

1251–52: "But wait till their arrival / Prompts us"—This line refers to the arrival of Clytemnestra and Aegisthus. The word translated as "arrival" often means "presence"; an ancient commentary tells us that in this context it means "right time" (*kairos,* as in 1259), which we have supplied in 1254 for the combination of two verbs meaning "is present" and "is fitting." So interpreted, Orestes' lines here would be another warning to Electra to tone down her rhetoric until they have had their revenge. Taken in the more usual way, however, this is a double warning, as if Orestes were to say: "Be quiet until they are here, then remember what they did—not by speaking or wailing, but by killing them."

It's always proper to speak out on this.
Till now I barely had the freedom to open my mouth.

ORESTES:
I entirely agree with you. So protect your freedom.

ELECTRA:
How?

ORESTES:
Stop trying to talk so much when it's not the right time!

ELECTRA:
But you are here, brilliantly! How could I react
With utter silence? It wouldn't be a fair trade.
I couldn't think, I couldn't hope
To see you. And now I do!

ORESTES:
You certainly do, now that the gods have goaded me into it.

ELECTRA:
O joy beyond joy,
If a god brought you to our house!
I declare that all of this
Is moved by a divine spirit.

ORESTES:
This joy of yours—I'd hate to cut it back,
But I am afraid it's too much. It's carrying you away.

(He starts to turn away from her.)

1256: "Till now . . . open my mouth"—An alternative translation, following Kells (1973), is "Just now I could hardly hold back from shouting freely," which takes the main verb (*eschon*) in its usual sense. We follow other editors, such as Lloyd-Jones (1994) and Jebb (1894).

1257: "So protect your freedom"—Orestes means that Electra should keep her outbursts in check. Otherwise, if she is overheard, she will lose the freedom of speech she hopes she has now won. See 1283.

1264: "Now that the gods have goaded me into it"—To what extent has Orestes been goaded by the gods? See note on 35–38.

A line is missing from the manuscripts after 1264, corresponding metrically to 1252. The traditional line count between 1265 and 1270 does not give us enough lines, but none are missing from the manuscripts at that point.

[Epode]

ELECTRA:
Don't!
It's been so long. You chose to come.
Your coming is so dear to me.
Don't! You see me full of sorrow.

ORESTES:
Don't what?

ELECTRA:
Don't take your face away from me.
You'd ruin everything. *(Trying to touch his face.)*

ORESTES:
I'd certainly be furious if anyone else took us apart.

ELECTRA:
So I may?

ORESTES:
Of course!

(They embrace.)

ELECTRA:
Dear one, when I had lost all hope
I heard a voice,
But I kept my passion without a voice.
I did not shout aloud when I heard it in my misery.
But now I have you right in front of me,
The face I love the most.
My troubles would never make me forget you.

ORESTES:
This is too much talk. Let it go.
You don't need to convince me that Mother's a bad woman
Or that Aegisthus is sopping up Father's wealth,
Pouring it out or sprinkling it around foolishly.
Your talk would hold us back from the time to act.
Instead focus on our current situation:
Tell me where we should show ourselves, or hide,
To complete our mission and wipe the smile
From our enemies' faces. And make sure Mother does not guess

The truth that we've come home. She mustn't see you
With a shining face. So pretend it's a disaster, as was reported,
And keep crying. When we have succeeded, then
You may be happy and smile as much as you like.

ELECTRA:
My brother, whatever you care about,
I will make that my care also. Every joy
I have I got from you, not on my own.
And I would not cause you the least bit of pain—
Even if it were of some great advantage to me.
That would be no way to serve the divinity
That is at work here.
Now, you know what's inside—
Of course you do. You heard Aegisthus is away
But Mother's home. No fear: She won't see me
With a smile or a shining face.
I've hated her for ages, in the extreme,
And now that I have seen you I can't stop
Crying out of happiness. How could I possibly?
One and the same road brought you to me, dead
And alive for me to see. You surprised me so much
That if Father walked in right now,
I would not call it a miracle. I'd believe I saw him.
Your coming brings me so much joy;
You must give me whatever orders you please.
If I were alone, I'd get one thing right out of two—
A noble way to save myself or a noble death.

ORESTES:
Please be quiet. I hear someone leaving
The house, coming our way.

ELECTRA: *(To Orestes and Pylades.)*
Go inside, you two.
It's important: No one at home could ward off the thing
You are bringing them, and they won't receive it with pleasure.

(Enter the Tutor through the great doors.)

1324–25: "The thing . . . bringing them"—the ashes of Orestes. Electra means to be overheard by whoever is coming through the doors. But, by a nice irony, she also means vengeance.

TUTOR:

You're being total idiots. Have you lost your minds?
Don't you care about your lives?
Were you born stupid?
The greatest possible danger is not around the corner;
It's right here on top of us now, and you don't realize it.
If I had not stationed myself just inside these doors
And been standing watch over you for some time,
Your plans would have gotten into the house before you did.
As it is, I have taken care to prevent that.
Now, you two, shut down this long conversation,
Put aside these endless exclamations of joy,
And go inside. At a time like this, danger is imminent,
And you must finish your business right now. It's time.

ORESTES:

So how will it be for me in there?

TUTOR:

Fine. It's settled that no one knows you.

ORESTES:

So you must have told them I am dead.

TUTOR:

As far as they know, you are in Hades.

ORESTES:

Were they happy about that? What did they say?

TUTOR:

I'll tell you when it's all done. For now,
Things are fine with them, even what's not fine.

ELECTRA:

Who is this, brother? For gods' sake, tell me.

1340: "It's settled that no one knows you"—This is what the manuscripts say. Lloyd-Jones (1994) and some others supply *me* (me) in place of *se* (you), so that the Tutor is assuring them that he himself hasn't been recognized. But this makes nonsense of 1341.

1345: "Things are fine . . . even what's not fine"—This line hints that Clytemnestra is delighted at the news of Orestes' death, so things are fine with her. But her being delighted is odious, so things are not fine. The Tutor does not want to spend any more words on this.

ORESTES:
You haven't guessed?

ELECTRA:
Nothing comes to mind.

ORESTES:
Don't you remember the man you gave me to once?

ELECTRA:
What? What sort of man?

ORESTES:
It was his hand
That guided me to the land of Phocis, as you wished.

ELECTRA:
Is this the man? The only one I found, out of all of them,
Who was faithful when Father was murdered?

ORESTES:
He's the one. Now, no more cross-examination.

ELECTRA:
You dear light! You are the only one who saved the house
Of Agamemnon. Could you really be here? Is it really you
Who saved him, and me, from all that trouble?
Your dear, dear hands! And your feet—
What delicious work they have done! You've been here so long—
How could I not recognize you? You killed me
By what you said. But what you did was joy to me.
Welcome, Father. You seem like a father to me.

1347: "Nothing comes to mind"—an unusual formation in Greek, appearing in the manuscripts. Lloyd-Jones (1994) follows a correction that translates this line into a more usual Greek expression: "I have never seen him." Here, more than before, Electra's emotions threaten to spoil her plan.

1359–60: "You killed me . . . joy to me"—Rhetoric of this period delights in the contrast of word and deed; the Tutor's words were devastating to Electra, but what he did with those words—deceive Clytemnestra—led to the happy result (for Electra) that Orestes has a clear path to killing Clytemnestra.

Welcome! You can be sure there's no one in the world
I hated so much and loved so much as you on the same day.

TUTOR:
That's enough. Our story, about after we left,
Will be told over many cycles of days and nights,
And you will know it all clearly then, Electra.
But I am telling you, while you're just standing around,
That the right time for action is now. Now Clytemnestra is alone;
Now none of her men are inside. If you let the moment go,
Keep this in mind: You will have to fight
More men than these, and they will be more cunning.

ORESTES:
We don't have time for so much talking. Pylades,
We need to go inside and get our job done quickly.
But first, let's greet the gods whose images are set
In front of Father's house.

(They pray silently.)

ELECTRA:
Lord Apollo, graciously hear their prayer,
And let me add my own to theirs.
My eager hands have made you many offerings
From whatever I might have. Lord of Light, Apollo,
I have little now to give. I beg, I entreat you on my knees:
Be our ally in these plans we've made, and show
All people how great a penalty the gods hand out
To those who trample on reverence.

(Exit Orestes and Pylades through the great doors, followed by the Tutor. Electra follows to the doorway so that she can see what takes place and report to the chorus.)

1379: "Lord of Light"—Sophocles may have in mind a different meaning of the word—"Wolfish" or "Wolf-slayer," referring to the myth that gave the agora at Argos its name. See note on 6.

Third Stasimon

CHORUS:

[Strophe]

Look! He is on the move, Ares,
Blasting gales of foul strife and blood.
Already the hounds have tracked their evil prey
Beneath the roof. They are inescapable.
Soon now my heart's dream
Will come true here on earth.

[Antistrophe]

Now the defender of the dead
Is being led on the silent feet of deception
Right to the center of his father's former wealth,
And the blood is ready for his hands.
Hermes, son of Maia,
Guides him in darkness,
Concealing the trick till now,
Waiting for this moment.
But he waits no longer.

ELECTRA:
My dear women, the men are at the very point
Of doing this thing, so keep it quiet.

CHORUS:
What are they doing now?

ELECTRA: *(Darting away from the doors.)*
She has the burial urn.
She's dressing it for burial. Those two stand near.

CHORUS:
But why did you rush back out?

1385: Ares—god of war and violence.

1395: "Hermes, son of Maia"—See 112. Hermes is both guide and trickster. He is a god of the deep earth, who guides souls down to the place of the dead. Maia is the eldest daughter of Atlas, associated with mountains.

ELECTRA:

I'm standing guard
So we'll know if Aegisthus starts to come inside.

CLYTEMNESTRA: *(With a shriek.)*

This house
Is full of killers! There's no one on my side!

ELECTRA:
Someone is shouting inside. Do you hear it?

CHORUS:
Yes, I heard it. I wish I hadn't.
Horrible. It made my flesh creep.

CLYTEMNESTRA:
I'm finished! Aegisthus, where are you now?

ELECTRA:
Listen! What a horrible scream!

CLYTEMNESTRA:

My child, O my child!
I gave you birth! Have pity on me!

ELECTRA:

But you had none—
There was no pity in you for the father who planted the seed.

CHORUS:
O city! O family!
What misery! Your days are coming to an end.

CLYTEMNESTRA: *(With a shriek.)*
I'm hit!

ELECTRA:
Hit her again! Make it twice if you're strong enough.

CLYTEMNESTRA:
Another blow!

ELECTRA:
How I wish Aegisthus had the same!

CHORUS:
Curses fulfilled! Drop by drop, the thirsty dead,

Alive beneath the ground, suck back the blood
Of those who killed them long ago.

(Enter Orestes and Pylades through the great doors. Their swords are bloody.)

[Antistrophe]

And here they are. His hand drips red
From a sacrifice to Ares.
I do not know what to say.

ELECTRA:
Orestes! How did it go?

ORESTES:
In the house,
It's good, if Apollo's oracle was good.

ELECTRA:
Is she dead? Miserable woman!

ORESTES:
You'll never be afraid again.
Mother's pride will not humiliate you any longer.

CHORUS:
Be quiet. I see Aegisthus.
He is very close.

ELECTRA:
Boys, you'd better go back.

ORESTES:
Where do you see him?

1422–23: The manuscripts assign these lines to Electra, but modern editors assign them to the chorus leader.

1423: "I do not know what to say"—following the manuscript reading. Almost all modern editors correct the text to read, "Nor can I find fault with it [the sacrifice]" (Lloyd-Jones 1994), putting *psegein* in place of *legein.*

1426: The manuscripts mistakenly assign this line to Orestes.

1427: Three lines—two of Orestes' and one of Electra's—are missing from the manuscripts.

ELECTRA:
He's coming home from the outskirts of town
Full of joy . . .

CHORUS:
Go quick to the entryway.
Do it now! Other things can wait.

ORESTES:
Don't worry, we'll finish the job.

ELECTRA:
Hurry up now; follow your plan.

ORESTES:
I'm going, I'm gone.

(Exit Orestes and Pylades through the great doors.)

ELECTRA:
I'll see to things out here.

CHORUS:
Speak gently in his ear, and don't say very much—
That would be best—so he'll dash blindly
Into the hidden toils of justice.

(Enter Aegisthus, quickly, through the stage left wing.)

AEGISTHUS:
Where are the visitors from Phocis? Which of you knows?
I heard they brought us news that Orestes had lost
His life in a chariot wreck.

(No one answers. They are trying to give Orestes time to get ready. Aegisthus singles out Electra.)

You! I choose you. Yes, you. Where's that rough tongue
You used to have?

(Electra still does not answer.)

This is largely your concern,
I think, so you should know the most. Answer my question!

1435: "Hurry up now; follow your plan"—the manuscripts wrongly assign this line to Orestes.

ELECTRA:

Of course I know. How could I forget
This catastrophe, this loss of my nearest and dearest?

AEGISTHUS:

So where might our guests actually be? Tell me.

ELECTRA:

Inside. They got to their hostess with ties of friendship.

AEGISTHUS:

Is it really true they brought news of a death?

ELECTRA:

No, not news, not mere words. They proved it.

AEGISTHUS:

So we can be sure, on the basis of visual evidence?

ELECTRA:

Of course you can. But it is not a happy sight to see.

AEGISTHUS:

For once, after all these years, you've said something that gives me joy.

ELECTRA:

Have your joy, then, if you enjoy these things.

AEGISTHUS:

Open the palace doors—I command it. And show
What's there to all the people of Mycenae and Argos,
So that if any of them have been hanging on empty hopes
For this man, now they'll see him dead.
Then they'll answer to the reins I pull, and they won't need me
To force them, through punishment, to grow some good sense.

1451: "They got to their hostess with ties of friendship"—a double case of double meaning. Orestes and Pylades "got to" Clytemnestra by killing her, but Aegisthus is to understand that they received a warm welcome from her. Ties of friendship are most commonly those of family. At the level Aegisthus is supposed to understand, the two young men have made a friend of Orestes' mother by bringing news of his death. But Electra means that they are family to each other, rather than guest and hostess. Jebb (1894) translates both double meanings together: "They have found a way to the heart of their hostess."

ELECTRA:
My part of that is finished; after so much time, I've got it—
My mind is sound. I've learned to serve those who are stronger.

(Attendants open the doors, and the ekkyklēma *inside—a wheeled platform—reveals the body, laid out in funeral wrappings. Orestes and Pylades stand over it. Aegisthus speaks at first without uncovering the face.)*

AEGISTHUS:
Zeus! What an apparition! This fall of the dice
Is due to some grudge of the gods—Nemesis, perhaps,
But I won't say that. Uncover its face. It's my kin.
Let it have the opportunity to be mourned by me.

ORESTES:
Use your own hands. It isn't my duty; it's yours
To look at this and speak to it like a close relative.

AEGISTHUS:
That's good advice, and I'll follow it. Now you:
Is Clytemnestra at home? If so, call her for me.

ORESTES:
She's very close to you. Don't expect her anywhere but here.

(Aegisthus uncovers the face of Clytemnestra's body.)

AEGISTHUS:
What the hell is this?

ORESTES:
Are you afraid of someone? Someone you don't recognize?

1465: "I've learned . . . stronger"—to work to the advantage of those who are either better or in power. (The Greek for "stronger" can mean either "better" or "more powerful.") Electra's words have a double meaning: Aegisthus thinks she means to serve him, but she means she is serving the gods, who are of course morally better than Aegisthus, as well as more powerful. The Greek is echoed in Plato's *Republic* by Thrasymachus' definition of justice as what serves those in power (338c2), where the same double meaning is in play.

1467: Nemesis—goddess of righteous vengeance. See 792.

AEGISTHUS:
Who are these men? What is this trap I've fallen into?
What a miserable throw of the dice!

ORESTES:
Didn't you notice awhile ago
That although you're alive, you've been matching words with the dead?

AEGISTHUS:
I see what you are saying. It has to be—
It can only be—Orestes who is talking to me.

ORESTES:
What a superb prophet you are! You missed it for ages.

AEGISTHUS:
I'm finished. It's horrible. But let me say something.
I'll be brief.

ELECTRA:
Don't let him speak another word,
For gods' sake, brother. He'd just draw things out.
When someone's in a tough spot, about to die,
What's the point of having more time?
Kill him right away, and when you've killed him,
Let whoever might take him give him a burial
Out of my sight. That is the only way,
After all these years of misery, that I'll be released.

ORESTES: *(To Aegisthus.)*
Go inside; hurry up. Words are not the issue
Any longer. It's your life that is at stake.

1478: "Although you're alive . . . words with the dead"—In other words, although you're alive, you've been addressing on an equal basis men you believe to be dead. Orestes leaves this implication unsaid: we are in fact alive, and you are now a dead man. This translation follows the original Greek text, with Lloyd-Jones (1994), a text that implies a threat against Aegisthus' life. Jebb and Kells follow a widely admired emendation that leads to one result or another that would be less frightening to Aegisthus: "that you have for some time now been addressing living men as though they were dead" (Kells 1973); "that the dead, as thou miscallest them, are living" (Jebb 1894).

AEGISTHUS:
Why are you taking me inside? If this is right, this thing
You're doing, why do it in the dark? Aren't you ready to kill?

ORESTES:
Don't give me orders. Go where you killed
My father so you can die in the same place.

AEGISTHUS:
Is it really necessary that this very house should see
The evils that come to Pelops' heirs, now and in the future?

ORESTES:
It will see yours. On that point, I am the top prophet.

AEGISTHUS:
You claim a skill your father did not have.

ORESTES:
You're talking back too much. You lengthen the road.
Get moving!

AEGISTHUS:
Lead on.

ORESTES:
You go first.

AEGISTHUS:
So I won't escape?

ORESTES:
No, so you won't
Find a pleasant way to die. I must make sure it hurts
Bitterly. This is justice for all: Kill them on the spot,
All of them who choose to violate the law.
Then there won't be so much crime.

(During this speech, he forces Aegisthus through the great doors, and at the end of it, he follows. The doors close.)

1498: "Pelops' heirs"—Aegisthus is begging for family sympathy (Jebb 1894). He, too, is a descendant of Pelops and has inherited an equal share in the curse. See House of Pelops Family Tree and note on 505.

1500: "You claim a skill your father did not have"—Agamemnon did not foresee his own murder, but Orestes claims to foresee Aegisthus' death.

CHORUS:
Seed of Atreus, how much you suffered
Before you won through to freedom—barely—
But perfectly now, from this beginning.

–END–

1508: "Seed of Atreus"—Agamemnon was a son of Atreus, so his heirs are descendants of Atreus. See House of Pelops Family Tree.

Selected Bibliography

Greek Text and/or Commentaries Keyed to Greek Text

Denniston, J. D. *Euripides:* Electra. Oxford: Clarendon Press, 1939.

Diggle, J. *Euripides Fabulae,* Vol. 2. Oxford: Clarendon Press, 1981.

Finglass, P. J. *Sophocles:* Electra. Cambridge: Cambridge University Press, 2007.

Garvie, A. F. *Choephori.* Oxford: Clarendon Press, 1986.

Jebb, R. C. *Sophocles:* Electra. Third edition. Cambridge: Cambridge University Press, 1894.

Kells, J. H. *Sophocles:* Electra. Cambridge: Cambridge University Press, 1973.

Lloyd-Jones, H., and N. G. Wilson. Sophoclea: *Studies on the Text of Sophocles.* Oxford: Clarendon Press, 1990a.

———. *Sophoclis Fabulae.* Oxford: Clarendon Press, 1990b.

Murray, G. *Euripides Fabulae,* Vol. 2. Oxford: Clarendon Press, 1913.

Paley, F. A. *Euripides: With an English Commentary,* Vol. 2. London: Whittaker, 1874.

Commentaries Keyed to Accompanying English Translation

Cropp, M. J. *Euripides:* Electra. Warminster: Aris and Phillips, 1988.

March, J. *Sophocles:* Electra. Warminster: Aris and Phillips, 2001.

Translations

Kovacs, D. *Euripides III* (Suppliant Women, Electra, Heracles). Cambridge, Mass.: Harvard University Press (Loeb Classical Library), 1998.

Lattimore, R. *Aeschylus I.* Chicago: University of Chicago Press, 1953.

Lloyd-Jones, H. *Sophocles I* (Ajax, Electra, Oedipus Tyrannus). Cambridge, Mass.: Harvard University Press (Loeb Classical Library), 1994.

Meineck, P. *Aeschylus:* Oresteia. Indianapolis: Hackett Publishing Company, 1998.

Meineck, P., and P. Woodruff. *Sophocles: Four Tragedies* (Ajax, Women of Trachis, Electra, Philoctetes). Indianapolis: Hackett Publishing Company, 2007.

Books and Articles

Bain, D. "[Euripides], *Electra* 518–44." *Bulletin of the Institute of Classical Studies* 24 (1977): 104–16.

Blundell, M. W. *Helping Friends and Harming Enemies: A Study in Sophocles and Greek Ethics*. Cambridge: Cambridge University Press, 1989.

Barrett, J. *Staged Narrative: Poetics and the Messenger in Greek Tragedy.* Berkeley: University of California Press, 2002.

Brown, A. L. "The Erinyes in the *Oresteia:* Real Life, the Supernatural, and the Stage." *Journal of Hellenic Studies* 103 (1983): 13–34.

Burkert, W. *Greek Religion* (trans. J. Raffan). Oxford: Blackwell, 1985.

Cropp, M. J., K. H. Lee, and D. Sansone, eds. *Euripides and Tragic Theatre in the Late Fifth Century.* Urbana: University of Illinois Press, 1999–2000. (*Illinois Classical Studies* 24–25.)

Csapo, E., and W. J. Slater. *The Context of Ancient Drama.* Ann Arbor: University of Michigan Press, 1995.

Davidson, J. F. "Homer and Sophocles' *Electra.*" *Bulletin of the Institute of Classical Studies* 35 (1988): 45–72.

Davies, M. *Poetarum Melicorum Graecorum Fragmenta,* Vol. 1. Oxford: Clarendon Press, 1991.

———. "Euripides' *Electra:* The Recognition Scene Again." *Classical Quarterly* 48 (1998): 389–403.

Dodds, E. R. "Morals and Politics in the *Oresteia.*" *Proceedings of the Cambridge Philological Society* 6 (1960): 19–31. Reprinted in Lloyd 2007, 245–64.

Easterling, P. E. *The Cambridge Companion to Greek Tragedy.* Cambridge: Cambridge University Press, 1997.

Foley, H. P. *Female Acts in Greek Tragedy.* Princeton, N.J.: Princeton University Press, 2001.

Fowler, B. H. "Aeschylus' Imagery." *Classica et Mediaevalia* 28 (1967): 1–74. Pp. 53–66 reprinted in Lloyd, M., ed., *Aeschylus.* Oxford: Oxford University Press, 2007, pp. 302–15.

Gantz, T. "The Aeschylean Tetralogy: Attested and Conjectured Groups." *American Journal of Philology* 101 (1980): 133–64. Reprinted in Lloyd, M., ed. *Aeschylus.* Oxford: Oxford University Press, 2007, pp. 40–70.

Goff, B. "Try to Make It Real Compared to What? Euripides' *Electra* and the Play of Genres." In Cropp, M. J., K. H. Lee, and D. Sansone, eds., *Euripides and Tragic Theatre in the Late Fifth Century,* pp. 93–105.

Goldhill, S. *Reading Greek Tragedy.* Cambridge: Cambridge University Press, 1986.

Gregory, J. "Euripides as Social Critic." *Greece & Rome* 49 (2002): 145–62.

———. "Euripidean Tragedy." In *A Companion to Greek Tragedy,* pp. 251–70.

———, ed. *A Companion to Greek Tragedy.* Malden, Mass.: Blackwell Publishing, 2005.

Hornblower, S., and A. Spawforth, eds. *The Oxford Classical Dictionary.* Third edition. Oxford: Oxford University Press, 1996.

Kitzinger, R. "Why Mourning Becomes Electra." *Classical Antiquity* 10 (1991): 298–327.

Knox, B. M. W. *The Heroic Temper: Studies in Sophoclean Tragedy.* Berkeley: University of California Press, 1964.

Lebeck, A. *The* Oresteia*: A Study in Language and Structure.* Washington, D.C.: Center for Hellenic Studies, 1971.

Lloyd, M. "Realism and Character in Euripides' *Electra.*" *Phoenix* 40 (1986): 1–19.

———. *Sophocles:* Electra. London: Duckworth, 2005.

———, ed. *Aeschylus.* Oxford: Oxford University Press, 2007.

Loraux, N. *Tragic Ways of Killing a Woman* (trans. A. Forster). Cambridge, Mass.: Harvard University Press, 1987.

Luschnig, C. A. E. *The Gorgon's Severed Head: Studies of* Alcestis, Electra, *and* Phoenissae. Leiden: E. J. Brill, 1995.

MacLeod, L. Dolos *and* Dikē *in Sophokles'* Elektra. Leiden: Brill, 2001.

Meier, C. *The Political Art of Greek Tragedy* (trans. A. Webber). Baltimore: Johns Hopkins University Press, 1993.

Page, D. *Actors' Interpolations in Greek Tragedy.* Oxford: Clarendon Press, 1934.

Parker, R. *Miasma: Pollution and Purification in Early Greek Religion.* Oxford: Clarendon Press, 1983.

Pelling, C. B. R. "Tragedy, Rhetoric, and Performance Culture." In Gregory, J., ed., *A Companion to Greek Tragedy,* pp. 38–54.

Prag, A. J. N. W. *The* Oresteia: *Iconographic and Narrative Tradition.* Chicago: Bolchazy-Carducci, 1985.

Rehm, R. *Greek Tragic Theatre.* London: Routledge, 1992.

Russell, D. A., and M. Winterbottom, eds. *Classical Literary Criticism.* Oxford: Oxford University Press, 1988.

Said, S. "Aeschylean Tragedy." In Gregory, J., ed., *A Companion to Greek Tragedy*, pp. 215–32.

Scodel, R. "Sophoclean Tragedy." In Gregory, J., ed., *A Companion to Greek Tragedy*, pp. 233–50.

Segal, C. "The *Electra* of Sophocles." *Transactions and Proceedings of the American Philological Association* 97 (1966): 473–545.

Seidensticker, B. "Dithyramb, Comedy, and Satyr-Play." In Gregory, J., ed., *A Companion to Greek Tragedy*, pp. 38–54.

Silk, M. S., ed. *Tragedy and the Tragic: Greek Theatre and Beyond*. Oxford: Clarendon Press, 1996.

Sommerstein, A. *Aeschylean Tragedy*. Bari, Italy: Levante Editori, 1996.

Stevens, P. T. "Sophocles: *Electra*, Doom or Triumph?" *Greece & Rome* 25 (1978): 111–20.

Taplin, O. *The Stagecraft of Aeschylus*. Oxford: Oxford University Press, 1977.

Wiles, D. *Greek Theatre Performance: An Introduction*. Cambridge: Cambridge University Press, 2000.

Winnington-Ingram, R. P. *Sophocles: An Interpretation*. Cambridge: Cambridge University Press, 1980.

Woodard, T. M. "*Electra* by Sophocles: The Dialectical Design." *Harvard Studies in Classical Philology* 68 (1964): 163–205.

———. "*Electra* by Sophocles: The Dialectical Design (Part II)." *Harvard Studies in Classical Philology* 70 (1965): 195–233.

Woodruff, P. "Justice in Translation: Rendering Ancient Greek Tragedy." In Gregory, J., ed., *A Companion to Greek Tragedy*, pp. 490–504.

———. *The Necessity of Theater: The Art of Watching and Being Watched*. New York: Oxford University Press, 2008.

Zeitlin, F. "The Motif of the Corrupted Sacrifice in Aeschylus' *Oresteia*." *Transactions and Proceedings of the American Philological Association* 96 (1965): 463–508.

———. "The Argive Festival of Hera and Euripides' *Electra*." *Transactions and Proceedings of the American Philological Association* 101 (1970): 645–69.